I0477101

The Character of Leadership

The Roadmap and Compass
That Guides You through
the Landmines of Management

David W. Reeves

iUniverse, Inc.
New York   Bloomington

Copyright © 2010 by David W. Reeves

All rights reserved. No part of this book may be used or reproduced by
any means, graphic, electronic, or mechanical, including photocopying,
recording, taping or by any information storage retrieval system
without the written permission of the publisher except in the case
of brief quotations embodied in critical articles and reviews.

iUniverse books may be ordered through booksellers or by contacting:

iUniverse
1663 Liberty Drive
Bloomington, IN 47403
www.iuniverse.com
1-800-Authors (1-800-288-4677)

Because of the dynamic nature of the Internet, any Web addresses or links contained
in this book may have changed since publication and may no longer be valid. The
views expressed in this work are solely those of the author and do not necessarily
reflect the views of the publisher, and the publisher hereby disclaims any responsibility
for them.

ISBN: 978-1-4502-1262-5 (sc)
ISBN: 978-1-4502-1264-9 (dj)
ISBN: 978-1-4502-1263-2 (ebook)

Printed in the United States of America

iUniverse rev. date: 03/25/2010

Dedication

Many thanks to the great and dedicated men and women who were part of the winning tradition of our agencies. Their commitment to our vision and mission was the primary element in our success.

Special thanks to Cynthia, Steffani, Jeff, Mel, and Chet for their invaluable help in editing and content review. Couldn't possibly have done it without you.

Epigraph

"What I do is exceedingly different. I treat my clients the way that I would want to be treated if the roles were reversed. Doing so, earns me the privilege of being totally referable."

Contents

Introduction

At the age of twenty-five, and after only eighteen months of sales experience, I was asked to fill an agency-management vacancy for an old, established life insurance company. Even though I had been successful at selling, I was relatively unprepared for that assignment and had serious reservations about my ability to succeed. These reservations stemmed from the company's outdated philosophies in evaluating potential managers: "If he's good at selling, he can lead and manage others, and teach them how to be successful." Or, "If he's a good speaker and has good people skills, he should be a good manager; he should be able to lead others." Such thinking isn't just outdated, it lacks logic.

During the next twenty-eight years, I learned that mediocre performance in management results from two main factors. The first is a failure to understand that leadership is the key to successful organizations, and the second is that real leadership is a verb, not a noun. Real leadership requires action and exceptional accomplishment in meeting goals and working with others. People skills are one of the essential ingredients found in successful leaders, and so is great salesmanship. But the primary factor in organizational success is the ability to lead. This ability has nothing to do with title, position, or the name on the door.

Most of us know this, but it is strange to observe that in the complicated world of corporate, government, or academic management selection, there is a widespread belief that a candidate's qualifications, experience, or good verbal skills will naturally lead to management success. This isn't always the case.

There are, of course, many success stories about those who have risen from the ranks of the field force to reach prominent, top management positions in their companies. But disappointments outnumber those success stories among the ranks of management trainees, whose "sharp," "good-at-selling" qualities never melded into management strategies that would command lasting respect.

This failure is due to the fact that the people involved in making hiring decisions don't always understand marketing or leadership, that they dub skills that are useful—but not essential—as "management material," and that they have no authentic experience upon which to gauge the qualifications of a management candidate.

My father-in-law used to say, "Advice is easy to give and seldom appreciated." The truth of that simple statement brings me to the purpose of this work. At first glance, you may ask: Why offer yet another treatise on the subjects of management and leadership, when so many writers have extensively studied the matter? Why risk killing more "sacred cows"?

Primarily, because what I have learned about managerial leadership (firsthand and through observing others' experiences) over more than twenty-eight years, may prove useful to top management in every company as well as field management in every industry.

I approach this potpourri of leadership principles with knowledge and inspiration. My knowledge is of things as they really are in the world of building successful organizations. And my inspiration stems from studying the lives of leaders who have accomplished greater things than most people dream about.

In my association with some of the most successful leaders in business, athletics, and academia, I have learned that successful leaders posses three common attributes:

First, each leader I observed demonstrated a significantly higher-than-average standard of performance. Second, they each had an exceptional leadership style and energy level. Third, almost all of them had tremendous people skills: they were both balanced and flexible in their interactions with others.

As a result of implementing such exemplary leadership styles and practices, our agencies were always among the leading agencies in our company. During the twenty-eight years that we were building successful agencies in two different states, we were the leading agency in the company ten times. In the other years, we were ranked either second or third.

We also received the prestigious Master Agency Builder Award, which gives industry recognition to the top one hundred agencies in the nation. The interesting thing about that award is that we earned it when there were "mega agencies" that covered whole states. Our little agency was nowhere near that size. We only had twenty-five to thirty agents, and our territory encompassed less than 40 percent of a very small state's population. As a result, we used to say that if size were the criteria for success, then Miss America would weigh four hundred pounds. Size is not the criteria, and our relatively small team of winners had a success ratio that was significantly greater than the average for our industry. Not only that, the ratio exceeded that of most large agencies in the state. How did we accomplish that feat?

The answer is found within the pages you are about to read. As you learn the difference between management and leadership, and as you arm yourself with the roadmap and compass that will identify the location of management landmines, you will evolve into the leader you've always wanted to be. You'll begin to find yourself among the best, most inspiring leaders you've ever known. And as that happens, you'll find a new ease and satisfaction that you've never quite been able to grasp in your work before. At that point, you'll be on your way to achieving greatness, in the mercurial business of successfully leading others and building a very profitable organization.

Chapter One

Do What The Best Are Doing

That which we persist in doing becomes easier for us to do, not that the nature of the thing itself has changed, but that our power to do it has increased.

—Heber J. Grant

Long before I became successful at agency building, I ran track for Brigham Young University. By the spring of 1966, my best time in the hundred was 9.5 seconds, which was good enough to win most meets in our conference, but it wasn't nearly good enough for me to be noticed in national meets.

Early in my senior year, I was sitting in the stands at a major national meet held in Southern California. I was feeling sorry for myself after having finished poorly in both the hundred and the two hundred races. Down in the infield sat Tommie Smith of San Jose State University; Tommy held the world record for two-hundred-meters, and was among the best in the world at one-hundred-meters. Though I had never met him, I went down to the infield, walked right up, and blurted out, "Tommie, I'm Dave Reeves from BYU, and I was

1

just wondering if you could tell me what it is you do every day?"

He said, "You mean my workout?"

I said, "Yes."

He told me to get something to write on. I did, and he began to write. He wrote down what he did on Monday, Tuesday, and every day of the week, including the day before the meet and the day of the meet. He told me how he warmed up and how he warmed down. Then he actually showed me the best thing of all: the "Sprint Form Workout," which he'd learned from his coach, the great Bud Winter.

I took that workout back to Provo, and on the following Monday, I began to do exactly what Tommie Smith was doing in his workout. My sprint coach didn't think much of it, mainly because it wasn't his idea, but I had tried doing it his way for two years and the results were less than spectacular.

Every week, I was getting just a little faster and a little better as my own "sprint form" improved.

Five weeks later, Tommie and the San Jose State University Track Team came to Provo. I was about to learn whether the metamorphosis of Dave Reeves was complete.

We were called to our marks in the one-hundred-yard dash. The gun went off, and I was out of there like a shot. At twenty-five yards, I had him by one foot. At fifty yards, I had him by one yard. At seventy-five yards, I had him by two feet. At ninety yards, I had him by one foot. At ninety-eight yards, he was right on my shoulder, and I could see him in my peripheral vision, which is when I made a bad tactical error and lunged for the tape. Those of you who have run track know that the lunge broke my stride, while Tommie, still in perfect form, leaned into the tape and beat me by three inches. We both ran that hundred-yard race in 9.3 seconds.

As we got to the end of the straightaway and turned to walk back, I said, "Nice race, Tommie."

He said, "Yeah, Reeves, nice race ... I didn't tell you everything, did I?"

Even though I lost that race, I learned a valuable lesson. By implementing what one of the best sprinters in the world was doing, I improved my time for one-hundred-yards by two-tenths of a second. At that speed I had crossed the finish line six feet ahead of where I had finished my races in the past. The results of changing the way I had been doing things prior to meeting Tommie, produced an improvement of two-tenths of a second. Two-tenths of a second makes the difference between world class and average college speed.

Although hard work is a key ingredient to success, it is not necessarily the primary element. Before talking to Tommy, I had already been working harder than the other sprinters on my team. After I armed myself with Tommy's workout, what changed was the refining of my technique. That was the primary element necessary for me to accomplish my objective.

In track and in business, I have seen many individuals fail in their pursuit of success, not because they weren't working hard, but because the way they went about achieving total success lacked that primary element, and they never knew it. Those individuals didn't need to work harder; they needed to learn how to refine their technique.

My purpose in sharing this story is not to impress you with my athletic brilliance, but rather to illustrate the point that in order to be the best, all you have to do is what the best are doing. Refining technique is not as simple as it sounds, because it requires change. Change, in turn, requires personal discipline, and in the maze of "quick fix solutions" in which we live, many individuals struggle with discipline. The truly great ones in both athletics and business are totally committed to following the roadmaps that are put forth by the real winners in their particular fields. They do so with integrity and without concern for how long it takes to accomplish the objective. By following such roadmaps, without wavering, the disciplined ones become the winners they emulate.

The trouble with such lofty ideals is that today's world gives little fellowship to the virtues of commitment, integrity, and discipline. Nevertheless, those who claim the prize of real greatness in what they do are successful because they are willing to do the things that the unfocused, uncommitted, and undisciplined will not do.

I'm reminded of a timeless presentation by Albert E. N. Gray, the former Vice President of Prudential Life Insurance Company. In that presentation titled *The Common Denominator of Success,* Gray said: "The common denominator of success—the secret of success of every man who has ever been successful— lies in the fact that he formed the habit of doing things that failures don't like to do."[1]

As you nod in agreement, perhaps you find yourself saying, "That's right!" Somehow, you always knew that was so, and this statement resonates within you.

My experience is that most great leaders have this uncanny habit of doing things that failures don't like to do. Not only that, but these leaders persevere without sacrificing any of the objectives they set out to accomplish in the first place. Somewhere along the way, as Gray said, they learned that the secret of every man and woman who has ever been successful is that they formed the habit of doing things that failures will not do. Gray went on to say:

"Perhaps you have been discouraged by a feeling that you were born subject to certain dislikes peculiar to you, with which successful men and women … are not afflicted. Perhaps you have wondered why it is that our biggest producers seem to like to do the things that you don't like to do. They don't! And I think this is the most encouraging statement I have ever offered [to any group]. But if they don't like to do these things, why do they do them? Because by doing the things they don't like to do, they can accomplish the things they want to accomplish."[1]

"Successful men and women are influenced by the desire for pleasing results. Failures are influenced by the desire for pleasing methods and are inclined to be satisfied with such results as can be obtained by doing things they like to do.

Why are successful people able to do things they don't like to do, while failures are not? Because successful people have a purpose strong enough to make them form the habit of doing things they don't like to do, in order to accomplish the purpose they want to accomplish."[1]

I discovered how true that was when I accepted a consulting assignment some years ago. At the time, the president of our company asked me to visit a young manager who couldn't seem to figure out why he and his sales team were unable to follow through on their goals.

When I visited with this young manager, trying to learn

his perspective on the problem, he said, "I don't get it. I work hard. I show up early, and I stay late. What am I missing?"

I told him that even though it appeared that he was working hard and long enough, I wondered if there was a lack of purpose in the whole process.

His response was, "I have plenty of purpose and so do the members of my team. We have families to take care of and lifestyles to support. Isn't that a good enough purpose?"

I told him that it wasn't, because it appeared to me that their purpose wasn't strong enough to make them form the habit of doing the things they didn't like to do. Simply said, it was easier for them to adjust to the hardships of earning an average living, than it was to adjust themselves to the hardships of making a great living. Quoting Albert Gray, I continued, "If you doubt me, just think of all the things you are willing to go without in order to avoid doing the things you don't like to do."[1] You have to realize that your current process is perfectly designed to give you the results you are getting.

To go back to the spring of 1966 when I was running track, the process I'd been implementing prior to meeting Tommie Smith had been perfectly designed to get the results I was getting—and I wasn't very happy about it. When I met Tommie and started doing what he did, my ability to compete at his level increased dramatically.

Emulating the best was not an easy concept for my young colleague to embrace, because it required him to follow principals that were new to him, and it also required him to excel in his management role at a faster pace than he had grown accustomed to. As I continued to mentor him in the things he needed to do to become successful, I introduced him to the profound words of Heber J. Grant: "That which we persist in doing becomes easier for us to do. Not that the nature of the thing itself has changed, but that our power to do it has increased."[2]

I told him that when this great truth became second nature to him, the things he needed to change would become less burdensome and a lot more rewarding.

And so it is with us. If we have a fire in the gut, the undying need to accomplish, a willingness to consistently do the things that successful people do, then the metamorphosis required to bring the desired results becomes easier.

But you must take care as you plan the necessary changes. Most of us have learned that meaningless plans promise failure, too much failure produces discouragement, and too much discouragement kills initiative. So be wise. Don't run faster than you're able, and don't try and do everything at once. Be patient with your process. Avoid negative self-talk and remember that the great ones you know have already gone through the pain you are now experiencing. That which you persist in doing really will become easier for you to do.

What if changing what you do seems unrealistic? What if the thought makes you say: "I guess I don't have what it takes." If that happens, you must step back, breathe deeply, and ask yourself if what you are doing looks anything like what the best are doing. If you cannot honestly say that it does, or if you really don't know what the best in your industry do, then you must find out who and where these people are and learn what makes them so successful. Doing anything else will put you on a path to mediocre results or even failure, where you will learn a new meaning to the words: "If you continue to do what you've always done, you'll continue to get what you've always got."

Are You Just Doing Good Enough?

Consider the opening lines from the poem *Good Enough* by Edgar A. Guest:

> My son, beware of "good enough,"
> it isn't made of sterling stuff;
> It's something any man can do,
> It marks the many from the few.

There's more to the poem, but the point of mentioning it is to clarify three things:

- Doing what you've always done is simply not "good enough."
- The term "good enough" suggests that just getting by is acceptable.
- Believing yourself "good" (in comparison to others who lead) is precisely what's holding you back.

The poem's concluding lines clarify that doing only the best is "good enough." Consider the final stanza:

> The flaw which may escape the eye …
> shall weaken underneath the strain
> and wreck the ship or car or train.
> For this is true of men and stuff
> Only the best is "good enough."

Over the years, I learned that this was not just a nice little poem. Instead, it describes the philosophy that motivates real leaders to accomplish their plans and goals.

I learned that it simply wasn't "good enough" to get by, to just take care of the basics. I learned that great accomplishment happens by being exceptional, and I applied the lessons learned in my role as the leader of our exceptional organization. It was never "good enough" for us to finish in the top three agencies for the year, because the plan was to finish first. Doing what the best were doing became part of the way we went about building the best offices in the company, and eventually, one of the best organizations in the industry.

The real world of business is considerably more challenging than it has ever been. The "just getting by" mentality doesn't make it today. Great organizations must evolve if they expect to win in business.

Here's the lesson:

- Hard work alone is not enough to achieve success.
- Technique refinement is the essential element, not just hard work.
- To be the best, emulate what the best are doing.
- You must form the habit of doing things that failures will not do.
- Your current process is perfectly designed for the results you're getting.

Chapter Two

Leadership Versus Management

Real leaders are ordinary people with extraordinary determination.

—Alexander Haig

I attended a national management conference a few years ago. The keynote speaker was Alden Porter, one of the most successful agency builders in our industry. He gave a talk entitled, "There Are No Heroes Anymore." Initially, I was bothered by the theme; I had a whole list of heroes that included the speaker. What was he talking about?

As that presentation continued, it became clear that Porter was talking about the dearth of leadership in society, in general, and particularly in government and business. He pointed to the general lack of leadership and integrity that we encounter often, questioning where men such as Washington, Adams, Lincoln, Churchill, and a host of others had gone. As I listened, I thought of what we had all learned in our history classes about the decline and eventual collapse of the Greco-Roman world in ancient times, and then the focus shifted from government to business.

Porter listed a handful of companies that had been caught in that downward shift from great leadership to the mediocrity of managing the status quo and how that loss of leadership had led to the failure of those companies. He spoke of how corporate greed and the decline of traditional moral values throughout the country provided painful evidence that the culture of basic goodness and virtue was declining.

That meeting was one of the defining moments in my career. It was then that I decided that having a "pretty good" organization was not enough. I decided to find and develop a group of individuals whose personal integrity and character would be strong enough for my vision to make big plans, set goals, follow through, and keep every promise necessary to accomplish those plans.

Not only would our people be men and women of high integrity, but I would provide the kind of leadership in this organization that would be contagious, challenging, and positive in its application. I determined that what my people would get from being part of such an organization would be very different from what others were getting in the typical business. Our agency would be founded on a simple mission statement: *"What I do is exceedingly different. I treat my client the way that I would want to be treated if the roles were reversed. Doing so, earns me the privilege of being totally referable."*

It may be that as you read our simple (some would say, sophomoric) mission statement, you might be rolling your eyes as you say: "Oh yeah, right! That's just the sort of naïve thinking that novices have when they first launch a new endeavor." Those who suffer from the cynical approach to building quality companies might also say, "In the real world of business, such lofty ideals cannot actually work over an extended period of time." If that's what you think, you're wrong; we lived our mission statement. Real leadership demanded it.

What we learned about why others take the cynical approach is that they are so involved in self-promotion and self-display that it is very difficult for them to embrace and sustain this simple, "others-centered" philosophy.

As you've seen, too many sales representatives, their supervisors, and their managers are wound up in strategies created only to make more money.

There's nothing wrong with being motivated by money, unless the motivation is so strong that one is willing to do and say whatever it takes to make that money. Therein lies the problem. If we don't have the personal integrity and the leadership initiative of putting the client's needs first, if we don't realize that the client gets top priority, which automatically assures that our financial needs will always be taken care of, then the whole process of building relationships with clients will break down over time. When that happens, the client loses, and ultimately, we lose too, because we lose that client. So instead of earning the right for our client to refer us to others, which would bring long-term success, we become "not referable" at all and are left to reinvent the wheel, over and over again.

As an organization, one of our agency's most satisfying accomplishments was that we did, indeed, become "referable." And in the world of selling anything, from computers to Mack trucks, becoming referable is the ultimate in building relationships of trust.

In the context of our client relationships, we learned that by making the transition from "me-centered" thinking to "others-centered" thinking, we had launched ourselves on the path to gaining thirty years of experience. Prior to that, our path had been of the kind that yields one year of experience repeated thirty times. The result depended on whether we were prepared to fully commit to the concepts we affirmed in our mission statement, or if we were just going to give them lip service.

Those who don't understand the difference between management and leadership wonder if personal mission statements actually make a difference. They really do, and I have seen the effectiveness of these mission statements, not only in the simple organizations that I was building, but also in most Fortune 500 companies, such as Ritz-Carlton, GE, Costco, and Home Depot. But one of the serious problems in business today is that there are still countless companies who have no formal, written, mission statement. If you and your associates do not already have one, it is vital that you create one now. Real leaders can more effectively lead when mission statements are in place.

Our mission statement was simple: "What I do is exceedingly different. I treat my client the way that I would want to be treated if the roles were reversed. Doing so, earns me the privilege of being totally referable."

As we developed our business plan to be the best at what we did, it was fascinating to observe how that timeless, prophetic truth, spoken by Albert E. N. Gray, was a principal part of the success formula we espoused: "Successful men and women *are influenced* by the desire for pleasing *results*, while failures *are influenced* by the desire for pleasing *methods* and are inclined to be satisfied with such results as can be obtained by doing things they like to do."[1] (Emphasis mine)

Why is it so?

Again, Gray provides the answer: "Successful people have a purpose strong enough to make them form the habit of doing things they don't like to do, in order to accomplish the purpose they want to accomplish."[1]

Because I believed this to be true, I knew that if my agency was going to be "exceedingly different," I would have to be "exceedingly different." I would have to help my people understand that there is a big difference between developing a plan for success and creating a vision of how to implement and maintain that plan.

Such vision is more than a list of strategies, budgets, and incremental steps. Truly great vision goes beyond intellectual content and incorporates emotional content as well. That perspective begins to grow and evolve into personal core values that never change. The development of such core values prepares us to properly lead others.

To be in charge, to be the manager, to have title and position, to have your name on the door does not earn you the right to direct the careers and the lives of those in your organization. The quest to earn that right requires leadership.

Title and position do not bring leadership to an organization, but being committed to resolving the needs of others (including every associate and every employee in the organization) will qualify us to lead. With that kind of commitment, we earn the right to expect loyalty from every single associate. That loyalty includes their "buy in" to the mission statement, their willingness to assume responsibility for their plans, and their long-term accountability to us.

Leadership and Acccountability

John M. Huntsman is the founder and chairman of Huntsman Corporation. From 1970 until 2005, his was the largest privately-held chemical company and America's biggest family-owned and operated business, with more than $12 billion in annual revenues. In his book, *Winners Never Cheat*, Huntsman relates a story about great leadership; he tells how he learned accountability during his younger days as a naval officer.

Huntsman said: "In spite of inspired vision, the purest of intentions, exemplary dedication, and great skill, success is never guaranteed. What's important is that the person in charge takes responsibility for the outcome—be it good, bad, or ugly. Surround yourself with the best people available and then accept responsibility."[3]

In his early twenties, Huntsman was a young naval officer aboard the USS *Calvert* in the South China Sea. It was there that he learned, firsthand, what real leadership meant.

On one occasion, the ships of that squadron were to rendezvous with naval ships from seven other nations. The *Calvert* was carrying the admiral—or in naval parlance, the Flag. Every ship followed the lead of the flagship.

At 4 a.m., Huntsman was the *Calvert's* officer of the deck. As a twenty-three-year-old Lieutenant Junior Grade (LJG), he still had much to learn about life; yet he had received the great responsibility of directing the formation of the ships during those early morning hours.

He ordered the helmsman: "Come right to course 335."

The helmsman shouted back a confirmation: "Coming right to course 355."

Huntsman thought all was well, but had not clearly heard the erroneous response; he had ordered "335" degrees, not "355." As a result, his ship made the incorrect turn, and the remaining ships followed. They were all off-course by twenty degrees, and the formation was in dangerous disarray.

Avoiding possible collisions caused a massive entanglement—and it was Huntsman's fault. Fortunately, no damage was done, except to his self-confidence. He felt a sense of ruin and failure. How could he have requested the helmsman's confirmation of his orders, have received an erroneous response, yet not have caught the discrepancy?

Learning of the debacle, the captain came running to the bridge and immediately took over, relieving an embarrassed and devastated young lieutenant. After several hours, the forty-two ships were realigned. Later, when the seas were calm and order had been restored, the captain called Huntsman to his cabin.

"Lt. Huntsman," he said, "you learned a valuable lesson today."

"No sir," the young lieutenant responded. "I felt a great sense of embarrassment, and I let you and every one of my shipmates down."

"To the contrary, lieutenant, now you will never again permit such an act to occur. This will be a life-long learning experience for you. I am the captain of the ship. Everything that happens is my responsibility. You may not have caught the helmsman's mistake, but I am responsible for it."[3]

John Huntsman learned then and there what it means to

be a leader. Even though the commanding officer was asleep, his actions were the captain's responsibility. He also learned another lesson: by reassuring a young lieutenant that he still had his captain's confidence, the latter had extended hope for the future.

So, in addition to the lessons Huntsman learned, what else does it take to be effective in the role of leadership? Over time we learned, first of all, that leaders do not give up easily. Second, leaders are very persistent. Third, leaders demonstrate expertise and the self-assurance that convinces others that they know what they're doing and are capable of guiding others. And because leaders have the gift of being able to convince others, they carry the burden of always doing so with great integrity.

Leaders somehow draw upon their own inner resources, but they also draw upon the resources of a much higher power than themselves. Whether they are Christian, Jewish, Muslim, or Hindu, they are aware that they rely on a power greater than themselves for guidance and wisdom. Leaders literally become a light to those who follow them. Leaders are flexible, adaptable individuals of high integrity and commitment, who constantly live by their convictions. They inspire others to do better and be better, and as a result, they cause others to become committed to excellence.

As Hugh Nibley, the renowned professor of religion and philosophy, so succinctly put it in a 1983 university commencement address: "Leaders are movers and shakers, original, inventive, unpredictable, imaginative individuals, full of surprises that discomfort the enemy in war and the main office in peace. Managers, on the other hand, are safe, conservative, predictable, conforming organizational men and team players, dedicated to the establishment … As the power of management spreads ever wider, the quality deteriorates, if that is possible. In short, while management shuns equality, it feeds on mediocrity. On the other hand, leadership is escape from mediocrity. True leaders are inspiring because they are inspired, caught up in a higher purpose, idealistic and incorruptible."[4]

Because effective leadership is an art, not a science, there are comparatively few who naturally possess the gifts of leadership. Consequently, it becomes difficult for them to see this management forest for its trees.

So how do people who are not blessed with the gifts that great leaders possess overcome their deficiencies? It seems like a relatively simple problem to resolve, but in fact, it takes great patience to go through the process of finding out what the best are doing, and then beginning to do what they do. But in the process of learning what the best are doing, beware of "quick-fix" solutions. There aren't any.

Do What the Best Are Doing

One afternoon, when I was a little more than a year into my new role as agency manager, I was reading about a young man who was just a couple of years older than me. He lived two hours south, and he'd achieved remarkable success in our business. It was amazing. Considering how hard I was working and what little I had accomplished compared to him, how was that possible? I was so taken with this man's story that I called him on the phone and asked if I could come and visit him. I wanted to find out what he was doing to achieve such phenomenal success. He was willing to share ideas, and so down I went.

When I arrived at his office, I was very impressed by the

setting within. All the trappings suggested "success." The way he dressed was right out of the magazine, "GQ." He was way ahead of my humble office and style.

We visited for about an hour and a half. He told me many valuable things, but one thing he said that stuck in my mind to this day was: "Before I became a pro, I acted like one, and by acting like one, I became one." I thought of my college days and my adoption of the Tommie Smith workout. Again, this great truth reinforced itself in my mind: "In order to be the best, all you have to do is what the best are doing."

The metamorphosis of my perspective on success in business had just begun; I would never be the same. It was a compelling and vital piece of the foundation I needed in order to accomplish my goal.

Some time later, I was sitting in a conference room, waiting for a meeting to start. On the wall behind the president's chair was a picture of a peacock. The inscription under the picture said: "How glorious it is, and also, how painful to be an exception." I understood, and I was committed.

Here's the lesson:

- What I do is exceedingly different.
- You must develop personal integrity that is strong enough to make and keep commitments.
- Have you earned the right for your customers to recommend you to a friend?
- Title and position do not bring leadership to an organization.
- Leaders become a light to those who follow them.

Chapter Three

Courageous Leadership

Courage is rightly considered foremost of all of the virtues, for upon it all others depend.

—Winston Churchill

What you already know about personal courage—a key virtue for one who leads—is that it is not easy to maintain. Our natural desire to be liked often compromises our ability to lead courageously. When that desire dominates, we become afraid to require our associates' participation in strategic planning, goal setting, and ongoing action. We feel reluctant to hold them accountable for what they said they would do. Simply stated, we lose our courage to act proactively, because we fear that such action will generate a dislike from our subordinates. Consequently, when those subordinates and associates are unwilling to "go for it," it may very well be because they sense that same unwillingness in us.

The reasons we fail to live up to what we say we'll do revolve around the natural tendency toward inertia, procrastination, and fear. Winston Churchill faced such challenges in the darkest days of World War II, when the Allies' military might withered. Yet, when faced with the daunting task of standing up to the enemy, his willpower, courage, and determination inspired a nation and changed the course of its military resolve.

In today's world, those tendencies are huge obstacles to success, because most individuals are unaccustomed to striving for excellence and are unwilling to pay the price for the success they seek. When people obtain average results, they feel frustration and disappointment. Likewise, there are further frustrations and disappointments that revolve around the persistence and dedication required to achieve great results. Yet, it is fascinating to note that most people find it easier to adjust to the frustrations of average results than to the thrill of great results.

It takes courage to escape from old ideas, old standards, and traditional ways of doing things. This is one of the chief elements in what we call capacity. If we do not dare to differ from our associates and mentors, we will never be great in our life's endeavors.

Brian Tracy, the chair and founder of Tracy International, a human resources company based in San Diego, is one of the leading authorities on the development of human potential and personal effectiveness. In his presentation to a national management group, he discussed the uses of courage and the crippling effects of fear. He said that fear, or the lack of courage, is more responsible for failure in management and in life than any other factor. It is always fear that causes people to hold back, to sell themselves short, and to settle for far less than they are capable of.

I believe that you surprise yourself and surpass your

previous accomplishments if you can get past the fear that interferes with the realization of your full potential.

While building great sales organizations, we learned that fear of failure is the single greatest obstacle to success, no matter what you're selling. That fear, coupled with the fear of rejection, stifles performance and inhibits expression.

I saw that truth up close as I recruited, trained, and educated countless individuals whose aptitude test scores, personalities, conversational abilities, and other outward gifts assured me that they were absolute winners. There were others, however, who suffered from both the fear of failure and rejection. I soon found that they had such a need for the approval of others that they would not put themselves into a position of being rejected.

Have you ever noticed how much time some employees spend in preparing illustrations that might sell, talking about how hard the business is, or looking for a consensus about what a lousy manager they have? These employees look for any other number of things that fill their time, so that they can avoid the sales activities that might generate a rejection.

In the early years, I found that one of the members of my own management team suffered from such fears. He agonized over this same fear of rejection which afflicted some of his agents. Consequently, he would avoid holding them accountable for assignments, sales results, and other requirements. He was afraid that the reporting interview would yield poor results, which would then lead to an inquiry as to what had happened and what was going to be done to accomplish the agreed-upon performance schedule. The associate manager feared the resulting conflict, which he tried to avoid at all costs, because he needed the approval of those he was assigned to lead.

By this time, I'd had my interview with him and learned that instead of conducting face-to-face interviews with assigned agents, he had simply collected the paper report only. He was now sitting in my office, prepared to discuss total results. But the result was not what we had planned. I asked him what the individual in question had said about his reasons for not accomplishing the objective, and it was only then that the fearful associate manager admitted that he had not conducted face-to-face interviews with his assigned people. When I asked how many joint calls he had made with each of his new sales associates, he would admit to very few, or none.

Why? Because of his own fear of being rejected by the client and having to face that fear in the presence of a subordinate. His fear of being rejected was compounded by the potential embarrassment that a younger associate might observe his inabilities, and his belief that he would lose credibility in his group. As you can imagine, that became a self-fulfilling prophecy.

I am happy to say that the above scenario was only a problem in the early years of agency-building, when I did not have the seasoning to properly select associate managers who possessed the qualities expected of real leaders.

As the years went by, my ability to select winners improved, and I rarely had to deal with such problems from my management team. I learned that developing the right individual to be a part of my management team was more important to the growth and success of my organization than developing the right sales associates.

The Fear of Failure

I'm grateful that I learned how to recruit the winners I was seeking, but what about those of you who are currently building your own team? What if there are people on your team who are unable to solve their personal battle with these fears? You might be surprised to know that more than 99 percent of adults experience both the fear of failure and the fear of rejection. Some antidotes for those fears include:

- The acquisition of knowledge. The more you know about something the less fear you'll have about using it or doing it.
- Actively develop courage by specifically doing the very thing that you fear.
- Understand that the opposite of fear is actually love, self-love, and self-respect.
- Regularly act with courage in fearful situations. "That which we persist in doing becomes easier for us to do. Not that the nature of the thing itself has changed, but that our power to do it has increased."
- Fears subside and lose their ability to affect your behavior and decisions when you talk with others who have conquered it and emulate their perspectives and attitudes. All you have to do is what the best are doing.

I was very fortunate to learn these things while I was still young in business. In those days, I had the same fears all people have. In spite of that, I'd make appointments with business owners by phone. When I got to their office, I'd take the elevator to their floor, get off, find the suite number, and then stand outside in the hallway, while carrying on this inner conversation with myself: "What are you standing out here for?"

"Well, if I go in there, he might throw me out."

"Out where?"

"Out here!"

"Where are you now?"

"Out here!" Then, I'd go in.

The point is that the personal development of courage is the first responsibility of leadership, and the second is to develop and instill courage in your associates. But we must begin with ourselves, because you can't give away something you don't have. You can only encourage others to the degree to which you experience and demonstrate courage yourself. You set the tone and determine the standard.

Think about what you've learned by experience and observation. Everyone is afraid of being rejected, of failing, of looking stupid, and of making a really costly mistake. Everyone you meet is afraid in some way, and usually in many ways. Mark Twain said, "Courage is not the absence of fear; it is control of fear, the mastery of fear. The brave person is the person who acts in spite of his or her fear, who faces the fear, feels the fear and moves forward..."[5]

I found that fears diminished and lost their power as we confronted them and moved toward them. Conversely, every time we backed away from a fearful situation, the fear grew and became more powerful. The only way that men and women can develop courage is to consciously and continuously make a habit of confronting fear.

You've probably had the experience that when you treat every fearful situation as a personal challenge and an opportunity to become stronger and more determined, you are able to do the thing you feared, and you're able to kill the fear. This is called the process of systematic desensitization; in other words, doing something over and over again until it holds no fear for you at all.

Years ago, as I was completing my undergraduate work, I took a class in American Literature. It was there that I read, for the first time, Emerson's *Essays on Self-reliance*. As I mentioned earlier, from those essays came that great quote about persistency. That quote was often paraphrased by Heber J. Grant, and reads as follows: "That which we persist in doing becomes easier for us to do. Not that the nature of the thing itself has changed, but that our power to do it has increased."[2]

Over the years, I learned that this is one of the most powerful statements ever, regarding self-determination.

Consider the quote if it were changed as follows: "If I persist in being positive and proactive, it will be easier for me to be positive and proactive. Not that the nature of being positive and proactive will change, but that my power to be positive and proactive will increase."

Now, consider the alternative: "If I persist in being negative and cynical, it will be easier for me to be negative and cynical, not that the nature of being negative and cynical will change, but that my power to be negative and cynical will increase."

We could continue to illustrate the countless uses of Emerson's great statement and interject any number of positive or negative thoughts or words into the quote. However you chose to develop this principle, when you are confident that you have it in place, teach it to your people again and again. It will make a major difference in their self-determination.

The key element for all of us in overcoming fear *is* the acquisition of knowledge. For example, Napoleon Bonaparte, whom most historians consider to be the greatest single leader who ever lived, had legendary courage. It was not vain or impetuous courage. Napoleon was famous for his focused commitment to detail, and for taking pains to study and thoroughly understand every military situation he ever encountered.

I love Napoleon's ability to learn everything that was necessary in order to gain victory, because, I found that the more we knew about what we faced, as we planned to become the best organization in the company, the lower our level of ignorance. The lower our ignorance level, the more courage and confidence we naturally gained. And so the more time we took to think through a situation, the more capable we were in dealing with the problems that arose.

Napoleon planned for every contingency. He considered and followed through to its natural conclusion every setback or possibility or defeat he might encounter, and then he prepared against it. To be caught unprepared for unexpected setbacks is a mark of weak leadership.

When you proceed in this manner, your courage and confidence will increase. It simply comes from thinking about what could go wrong long before it does.

The failure to do so opens you and others up to fear, panic, and confusion if something does go wrong. Your ability to deal with such crises is the genuine test of courage and effectiveness in a leader.

"Remember, worry is merely a sustained form of fear caused by indecision. The only real antidote to worry is purposeful action. When we got busy doing something about the situation at hand, we didn't have time to worry. Taking action gave us the confidence, courage, and sense of control that wiped our fears away."[6]

Metamorphosis

Most people don't get where they want to go because they are impatient with the rules that are required to get there—such as learning everything about your own and about your competitor's business. But to do less promises disappointment and frustration. You may have already experienced that.

"That which we relentlessly persist in doing" actually does become easier for us to do. But the keyword is *persist*. Persistency cannot be maintained without courage and the willingness to pay the price to accomplish the goal. This is the very thing that failures will not do, because it takes courage to change the way you do things.

No one really wants to change. It's not comfortable. But it's as simple as it sounds. In order for a person to change, it is not enough that there be a great *desire* to change. We are aware of people, in parts of Africa, who have desire for food, and yet, who are starving to death. The desire for food is not enough to provide the food. It is the same for you in your desire to change. Simply said: In order for a person to change, **they must change**. There is a personal evolution required that is both real and painful. The resulting change brings that rare commodity—courage. Courage is a rare commodity, but its development within you and its incorporation into your leadership style is an absolute requirement. The success you seek is something that you attract by becoming the person you always wanted to be.

It is a great tragedy when those who have a vision of what they want to do and be cannot maintain persistency—the persistence necessary to overcome their bad habits and lack of courage. Consequently, such individuals are not able to pull themselves to a higher vantage point, where they can begin to see the rewards that await those who have the integrity and courage to change the things that must be changed.

Here's the lesson:

- Our natural tendency to be liked often compromises our ability to lead.
- Fear is more responsible for failure in management than any other factor.
- The step-by-step personal development of courage is the first responsibility of leadership.
- That which we persist in doing becomes easier for us to do.

Chapter Four

What We've Got Here Is A Failure To Communicate

The significant problems we face cannot be solved at the same level of thinking we were at when we created them.

—Albert Einstein

This chapter's title—derived from the movie *Cool Hand Luke*—has become a classic line that is true in far too many organizations. Through the years, one of the things we've tried to do with our associates was to ensure frank and open lines of communication. If my door was open, my associates knew that I welcomed the opportunity to hear what was on their mind; anyone could come in and ask for help, register a complaint, or make a suggestion. If there was a realistic solution available, we would try to implement it. Many of our more creative marketing plans came from our associates, and I was anxious to hear their contributions. Yet when I visited colleagues in other offices of the company, I was always surprised to learn that most of them never welcomed such discussion; instead, they held themselves aloof and were somewhat non-communicative.

Back in 1977, the American Marketing Association magazine

printed a classic piece titled "The Ill-Informed Walrus." The story is as priceless today as it was then, and it makes a great point about open and frank communication:

"'How's it going down there?' barked the big walrus from his perch on the highest rock near the shore. He waited for the good word.

Down below, the smaller walruses conferred hastily among themselves. Things weren't going well at all, but none of them wanted to break the news to the Old Man. He was the biggest and the wisest walrus in the herd, and he knew his business—but he had such a terrible temper that every walrus in the herd was terrified of his ferocious bark.

'What will we tell him?' whispered Basil, the second-ranking walrus. He well remembered how the Old Man had raved and ranted at him the last time the herd caught less than its quota of herring, and had no desire to go through that experience again. Nevertheless, the walruses had noticed for several weeks that the water level in the nearby Arctic Bay had been falling constantly, and it had become necessary to travel much further to catch the dwindling supply of herring. Someone should tell the Old Man; he would probably know what to do. But who? And how?

Finally, Basil spoke up: 'Things are going pretty well, Chief,' he said. The thought of the receding waterline made his heart heavy, but he went on: 'As a matter of fact, the beach seems to be getting larger.'

The Old Man grunted. 'Fine, fine,' he said. 'That will give us a bit more elbow room.' He closed his eyes and continued basking in the sun.

The next day brought more trouble. A new herd of

walruses moved in down the beach, and with the supply of herring dwindling, this invasion could be dangerous. No one wanted to tell the Old Man, though only he could take the steps necessary to meet this new competition.

Reluctantly, Basil approached the big walrus who was still sunning himself on the large rock. After some small talk, he said, 'Oh, by the way, Chief, a new herd of walruses seems to have moved into our territory.' The Old Man's eyes snapped open, and he filled his great lungs in preparation for a mighty bellow. But Basil added quickly, 'Of course, we don't anticipate any trouble. They don't look like herring-eaters to me. They're more likely interested in minnows, and as you know, we don't bother with minnows ourselves.'

The Old Man let out the air with a long sigh. 'Good, good,' he said. 'No point in our getting excited over nothing then, is there?'

Things didn't get any better in the weeks that followed. One day, peering down from the large rock, the Old Man noticed that part of the herd seemed to be missing. Summoning Basil, he grunted peevishly, 'What's going on, Basil? Where is everyone?'

Poor Basil didn't have the courage to tell the Old Man that many of the younger walruses were leaving every day to join the new heard. Clearing his throat nervously, he said: 'Well, Chief, we've been tightening things up a bit. You know, getting rid of some of the dead wood. After all, a herd is only as good as the walruses in it.'

'Run a tight ship, I always say,' the Old Man grunted. 'Glad to hear that all is going so well.'

Before long, everyone but Basil had left to join the new

herd, and Basil realized that the time had come to tell the Old Man the facts. Terrified but determined, he flopped up to the large rock. 'Chief,' he said, 'I have bad news. The rest of the herd has left you.'

The Old Walrus was so astonished that he couldn't even work up a good bellow. 'Left me?' he cried. 'All of them? But why? How could this happen?'

Basil didn't have the heart to tell him, so he merely shrugged helplessly. 'I can't understand it,' the old walrus said, 'and just when everything was going so well.'

Moral: What you like to hear isn't always what you need to know."[7]

Communication 101

What any of us likes to hear isn't always what we need to know. The funny thing is that most of us know this and have heard it all of our business lives. But isn't it strange that many of those who are in a leadership role apparently wear blinders to filter news? They either demand to hear only good news, or they need a very measured version of bad news, rarely, if ever, allowing an opposing viewpoint. It's as if hearing bad news would impede the communications process.

Some people question, "So what?" Well, if a leader's management style is either so fearful or so autocratic that the only acceptable input is positive input (no matter what the reality is) then that individual is living in a fantasy world, and communication often gets stifled in that world.

However, in the real world of building people and business, there's a problem with this style of management; sooner or later, reality reveals itself. And often, like the "Ill-Informed

Walrus," those who run their organizations are left feeling bewildered about their failed plans, and they wonder, "How could this happen to me?"

So what should leaders do if this is their management style and they don't know it? What should you do if you're in that situation? The only way to find out whether or not yours is the "walrus style" is to ask your best employee or associate—whom you know to be painfully frank and honest—to tell you if you have the "blind spot of the walrus." This is tough to do for those whose need for ego massaging (a common trait in far too many executives) is a major part of their sense of well-being. But if you don't ask for the honest opinion of a co-worker you trust, you probably will never get it elsewhere, and it may cost you the ultimate success you seek.

I knew a corporate CEO who suffered from a syndrome that was akin to the walrus's. Although this CEO had unquestionable integrity, he had surrounded himself only with those whom he believed agreed with his management style and perspective. Who could blame him? Who wouldn't want a management team that was easy to work with and willing to do the boss's bidding with no opposition? But in this CEO's case, he stifled any point of view that differed from his own. His myopia killed the synergy of the group, which in turn impeded the company's long-term growth and success.

In his book on leadership, Ken Shelton said that synergy can be created in an organization that values differing points of view. "Synergy results from valuing differences, from bringing different perspectives together in a spirit of mutual respect. Mature people view differences as potential strengths. They not only respect those with different views, they actively seek them out. They also seek objective feedback from both internal and external sources on their performance, products, and services, and look for ways to build complementary teams where the strength of one compensates for the weaknesses of another."[8]

Because of his real lack of maturity in his CEO role, his poor communicative skills, and his fear of conflict, my friend missed hiring a marketing vice president who was uniquely qualified in the complexities of building successful marketing organizations. Not only that, but the candidate possessed certain gifts that were extremely valuable in the recruiting and selection process, which is the lifeblood of all business organizations. He had the ability to motivate groups that far exceeded what most of his peers were able to do. He was strong, forthright, and when he spoke he was eloquent. He was never shy about speaking up on issues that needed to be questioned or clarified. He was, as Nibley said, "... a mover and a shaker, original, inventive, unpredictable, imaginative, and full of surprises ..."[4]

Because this prospective leader did not fit the mold of those who were already part of my friend's top-management team, he wasn't hired. The reason? The CEO feared that this candidate was too strong to become an effective member of that team. But this corporate management team was staffed, with one exception, by management types who opted for safe, conservative, predictable policies. They were conforming, organizational "yes-men" and team players who were dedicated to the establishment.

Did it matter? Well, I know this: today, that company is having serious problems establishing new, profitable regional offices and retaining its best and brightest. At the field level, the needed "success culture" does not filter down from the top as it might have, if my friend had appointed that unique candidate to the right position. My friend, who is a good man, was unwilling to listen to those who counseled him to make the right hiring decision. What he needed to know was not what he wanted to hear, and it cost him more than he could imagine.

He learned the hard way that the ability to communicate effectively is not a one-way street. The key to effective communication is to invite several points of view and then to listen carefully. Effective listening, without any predisposition to answer quickly, is as important as the ability to speak and be understood. One gains the ability to do both by giving up ego and seeking the advice and direction of those who have strengths one does not have.

Those who have difficulty with such processes often lack the personal resolve necessary to listen with great care, while maintaining the personal integrity to not get pushed around by the strength of others. When you have that strength, you earn greater credibility and bring a synergy to your business and relationships that cannot be gained otherwise.

Here's the lesson:

- What you like to hear isn't always what you need to know.
- Synergy results from valuing differences.
- Mature people view differences as potential strengths.
- The key to effective communication is to invite several points of view, and then to listen carefully.

Chapter Five

What I Do Is Exceedingly Different

Do what you love, love what you do, and deliver more than you promise.

—Norman G. Levine

As far back as I can remember, I have had this great need for order. Not to the point of being obsessive compulsive, but I was kind of a neat-nick. I followed the adage: "a place for everything, and everything in its place." The top of my desk was always straight and orderly. I worked out of a day-timer and listed every appointment and activity for the day, then checked it off as I completed it. If I missed something, I moved it forward to the next morning for immediate follow-up. I believe that the secret to getting things done is to do them now. I loved systemization, order, and precision, and I hated surprises—not the kind of surprise you get when someone sends you a gift or pays you a compliment, but rather the kind of surprise you get when someone fails to complete an assignment after promising they would, or the kind of surprise you get when someone tells you something is so, but then you learn later that they lied to you.

Consequently, I applied my need for order and my no-nonsense approach to accountability, to create a mental picture of the new associate we sought listing the attributes and skills the ideal candidate should possess. Unlike some agencies in our industry—whose managers were willing to hire almost anyone—we determined that we would accept *no* company-imposed recruiting quotas. We were determined to hire only a particular kind of individual.

We sought a self-starter, self-motivator, and self-disciplinarian who was motivated by money and could "go easily to people." Additionally, we were seeking a sharp individual, who would be filled with integrity and driven by the need to somehow make a difference. Our ideal candidate would have to be someone who had strong family ties and whose character was beyond reproach. In those days, few of my colleagues visualized the new associate they sought. Instead, they were willing to hire almost anyone who talked good, looked good, and smelled good.

Our recruiting process was designed to help us discern exactly how sharp and disciplined our new recruit was. That process included three different interviews, an aptitude test, and an assignment to personally interview twenty-five friends, relatives, or business associates.

We wanted to know if our new recruits were the kind of individuals that we would feel comfortable inviting to dinner in our own home. We also wanted to know if their style and personality would fit well in our existing organization, and we wanted to be able to determine whether we would be proud to introduce them to any of our existing clientele. We were very protective of our reputation throughout the state, and we wanted to be sure that the people we hired would represent us well to business owners and private individuals in the community.

Blueprint for Recruiting Winners

If you intend to have exceptional recruiting results, make sure that the individual you hire has all of the following attributes:

- Self-starter
- Self-motivator
- Self-disciplinarian
- Motivated by money
- Can go easily to people
- Sharp and filled with integrity
- Has solid family values
- Character beyond reproach
- Needs to make a difference
- Their style and personality fits well in our existing organization.
- They would be easy to introduce to our best clients.

How, you might say, is it possible to find such people? Every organization wants to add "winners" to the group, and we liked adding a certain kind of person to the group who would represent us well and help us maintain our reputation, both within the company and in the community.

But when you're just getting under way, or if you've just "cleaned house" in your quest to start doing what the best are doing, how do you find these people?

You start by making sure that "your own house is in order." If the high integrity, self-disciplined individual, described above, is not a pretty good picture of you, you must figure out in a hurry if you are willing to pay the price for such personal excellence. Remember, you cannot attract that which you are not.

If you are striving as hard as you can to be the kind of person you seek, you must begin to network with others. If you have just one person in your organization who fits the criterion listed, that one person can be a great center of influence for you.

Early in the development of our organization, even though most of our people had not developed into the "total package" described above, we did have one exceptional individual who was anxious to refer us to a couple of other winners. They, in turn, introduced us to others, and eventually, we'd hired a number of quality people, who started to bring others (who walked and talked just liked they did) to our organization.

Early in my career, I only had a couple of real winners in my group. As I shared this picture of the person I sought with them and explained my philosophy, it was fascinating to see how willing they were to suggest the names of others to me.

Those initial conversations went something like this. "John, I need your opinion on something. You've seen that our approach to recruiting new associates is a little different from what others in the industry are doing. Consequently, in our quest to add a couple of new, highly qualified associates to our team this year, we are looking for people like you, who are truly exceptional." Next, I would reiterate the list of attributes I've established above and ask John if he knows one or two people who fit that description.

At this point, some of you may be saying: "I never approached recruiting new people that way, and we've had a lot of success over the years."

To that I say, "If it ain't broke, don't fix it." But to those who haven't been successful at recruiting dedicated, professional individuals of high integrity, or if your recruits didn't develop into significantly productive people, take time today to determine what kind of an organization you want and begin to write your personal mission statement, with an eye toward the picture you've created. Until you're committed to hiring only that kind of person, you'll always get relatively disappointing results in your recruiting. Your mission statement will be the roadmap for establishing your recruiting process.

I mentioned earlier that our mission statement was really pretty simple. It said: "What I do is exceedingly different. I treat my client the way that I would want to be treated if the roles were reversed. Doing so earns me the privilege of being totally referable."

If you're wondering what our mission statement has to do with the list of attributes described in our 'Blueprint for Recruiting Winners,' the answer is: Our mission statement is based on a rather lofty premise that is not typical of most organizations. In order to develop and maintain a culture of *winners* who can adopt the mission statement as their own, the attributes found in the "blueprint" are essential.

When you're satisfied that your own mission statement is worthy of emulation, then share it with others in your group and have them create their own. When they have done that, get everyone together and ask for input as to what the company or organizational mission statement should look like. Once you have all that information, take it and carefully extract the best things from it. As you do that, ask yourself whether your mission statement is strong enough to inspire and lift the people in your organization to do better and greater things than they have ever done before. When they are fully invested in the company mission statement, then they will be motivated to help build the company by bringing people they know who fit the picture you've prepared for them.

If you are inspired by what you've prepared, the winners in your organization will be, too, and you will begin to attract more individuals such as the one described above.

Whether or not you're a frequent traveler, you may have heard of one of the world's best hotel corporations, the Ritz-Carlton. What makes this corporation stand out? Their mission statement. Not only that, but each department has one. You wouldn't be surprised to know that each hotel within the corporation and every department in each hotel have a mission statement; so does every employee. The corporate mission statement is simple and succinct: "Our mission is to satisfy the unexpressed wishes and desires of our guests."

One of my good friends is the management guru and

bestselling author, Stephen Covey. He tells the story of arriving late, due to flight difficulties, at a particular Ritz-Carlton, where he was scheduled to speak the next day to a management group. At check-in, he inquired about the closing time for room service. The desk clerk apologetically explained that room service had closed ten minutes earlier, but said that just as soon as Covey's check-in was concluded, he would go to the kitchen and make him a nice sandwich and some soup. Stephen protested, but the desk clerk said: "Mr. Covey, it is my job to make sure that your stay with us is as comfortable and memorable as possible. Please allow me to serve you."

Covey consented and went to his room to unpack. In about ten minutes, there was a knock at the door; it was the desk clerk. As promised, he had prepared a nice sandwich and a bowl of chowder. He again apologized that room service was not open. You can imagine how Covey felt about that kind of "above and beyond the call ..." service. You can imagine how you would have felt.

The next morning, during a break in his presentation, Covey found he needed new markers. Stepping out into the hall, he looked around, wondering where he could get new markers. Down the hall came a bell-boy. "Mr. Covey, is there anything I can do to help you?"

"Yes," he said, "I need some new markers for my white board."

"Not a problem, Mr. Covey, I will solve your problem. I'll be back in five minutes with those markers."

How is it possible that those two Ritz-Carlton employees, in separate, unrelated instances displayed a similar concern for my friend's needs? Where in the job description of a front desk clerk does it tell him to take time to fix a sandwich for a late guest? Isn't his job to just check people into the hotel? Isn't he going to get his same hourly or monthly wage, whether or not Stephen Covey gets room service after a late arrival? What about that bell-boy whose job description clearly states that he is to assist guests in getting their luggage to their room on time? Bell boys aren't responsible for procuring erasable markers, that's the job of some other employee. What's happening at the Ritz-Carlton Hotels?

What's happening is that the corporate, the hotel, the department, and the personal employee mission statements are all in alignment with one common goal. That goal is to make sure that every Ritz-Carlton guest leaves saying, "That was a pleasure; I'll be back." These employees, and the departments in which they work, have bought into the corporate mission statement. It is remarkable to see how two employees had the *self-motivation* to live that mission statement.

It was so with our best people. They, too, bought into our mission statement. "What we do is exceedingly different ..." was created to help our people treat their clients in such a way that those clients would leave our office saying, "That was a pleasure; I'll be back."

I believe that if other companies were to adopt the Ritz-Carlton mentality, they could significantly improve their bottom line. An "others-centered" mission statement that spreads throughout an organization will truly focus on the needs of the customer. It is disappointing to see that in corporate America, there is generally an apathetic response to the needs of the customer. One gets a picture that the unwritten, unspoken mission statement of far too many of these companies is, "This would be a great place to work, if it just weren't for customers."

We also see and feel the results of this cavalier attitude toward customer relationships in both academia and government agencies. At the core of this attitude is a combination of myopia, apathy, and turf protection. Such organizational blindness is the antithesis of the mentality prevailing in companies that are determined to do better than anyone else.

I have wondered whatever happened to the great service we used to get, years ago, on some of the major airlines. I wondered about that the last time I flew out of Atlanta, and Delta lost my reservation. But instead of making me feel like they felt bad about it and were really going to do whatever it took to fix the problem, their curt, annoyed attitude gave me the feeling they were quietly saying: "This would sure be a great place to work if it just weren't for customers." Ironically, as I waited for them to try and figure out my problem, I was reading an article by Jeff Benedict, printed in the *Boston Herald*, about the problems JetBlue had experienced in January 2007.[9]

The essence of the article was that JetBlue Airways had made headlines that January, experiencing the worst operations breakdown in its seven-year history, which led to more than 1,000 canceled flights. The bad news was countered with the way their former Chief Executive, David Neeleman, responded to the crisis, bending over backward to admit failure, accept responsibility, apologize, and compensate customers for their inconvenience.

Everyone, from public relations experts to aviation analysts, praised Neeleman for doing things that were largely unheard of in his industry.

Experience tells us that most chief executives would have ducked for cover or sent in a spokesman. Instead, Neeleman appeared on Letterman's show and said, "I'm not making excuses. We made a mistake. We put our crew members and our customers through hell, but we have solutions for this."

The next day, he appeared on several morning news shows, apologized, and unveiled a Customer Bill of Rights, guaranteeing compensation to passengers whose flights had been canceled. He admitted being totally mortified and humiliated.

Humility doesn't come easy to chief executives, as we know from recent corporate scandals. This is where Neeleman's personal faith made a difference.

This chief executive didn't let pride prevent him from publicly admitting mistakes and asking forgiveness. It also explains his habit of frequently serving as a flight attendant or a baggage handler for his company's flights.

Beginning at age nineteen, Neeleman spent a couple of years serving a mission in the slums of Brazil, where he learned to speak Portuguese. He also learned what it feels like to serve people who are less fortunate. This experience was a key influence on Neeleman's vision to create JetBlue; it armed him with a perspective that the customer is king.

It was a simple reflex for Neeleman to make his Customer Bill of Rights retroactive, so that it would cover all passengers who had been inconvenienced by those winter storms—a decision that cost his company approximately $30 million dollars.

The profound thing about Neeleman is that when this crisis struck, he asked himself: "What is the right thing to do?"[9]

It kind of makes you wonder if Neeleman ever worked for Ritz-Carleton, and gained the "customer first" mentality. Maybe his personal mission statement includes the phrase, "what I do is exceedingly different." If that line was not in his mission statement, he surely acted like it was. He delivered a lot more than promised.

Here's the lesson:

- The person you seek is a self-starter, self-motivator, self-disciplinarian, and can go easily to people.
- That high-integrity, self-disciplined individual must also be descriptive of you.
- You cannot attract that which you are not.
- Make sure that your clients are leaving your office saying, "That was a pleasure; I'll be back."

Chapter Six

The Excellence Paradigm

Be an Island of excellence in a sea of mediocrity.

—Stephen R. Covey

In the early 1960s, one of the world's great runners was Peter Snell, from New Zealand. He held the world record at 800 and 1,500 meters. At the 1960 Rome Olympics, he won the 800 meters. Four years later, at the Tokyo Olympics, he not only won the 800 meters again, but also won the 1,500 meters. He was the first man ever to win both events in the same Olympics. In addition to his great accomplishments, Snell is also respected internationally, not so much because of what he achieved, but because of how he achieved it: with total dominance, grace, humility, and dedication.

Prior to the Tokyo Olympics, *Sports Illustrated* sent one of their writers to New Zealand to interview Snell. When the writer arrived, he rented a car and drove out to Snell's home on the sea coast. It was lightly raining when he reached the house. Knocking on the door, the writer was greeted by Snell's wife, who told him that her husband was not in, but was out on the beach, running.

The writer thanked her and walked around to the back of the house toward the shore. As he walked across the sand, he could see the figure of a man running about a quarter of a mile to his left. As the runner got closer, the writer could see it was Snell, who waved as he passed, and kept on running. The writer watched as Snell nearly disappeared down the beach to his right. Finally he returned, and the two walked back to the house.

After changing and drying off, Snell sat down and the writer asked his first question. "Peter, please tell me why you were out there, on a day like today, running on the sand, in the cold and the rain?"

"I'm out there," Snell answered, "on a day like today, running on the sand, in the cold and rain, because I know that all my competition is inside, keeping warm."

It was lost on none of us that Peter Snell was the best in the world, not only because he knew what he wanted, but because he was willing to do the things that were required to get there.

He was willing to do the things that the less committed were unwilling to do. Such an "excellence" mentality was inspiring then, and it inspires today.

Dr. David T. Porter, an internationally prominent NCAA tennis coach who has numerous national titles and has trained countless All-American players, gave a lecture in 2007 where he invited his audience to consider a broader understanding of the word *excellence*. In that presentation, he delved into the deeper meanings and significance of the Greek word *arête`*, which is commonly translated as "virtue" or "excellence."

In his lecture, Porter identified the distinguishing

characteristics typical of those living in the twenty-first century, as compared to those who lived in ancient times. The first characteristic he identified in his contemporaries is the belief that success requires specialization, something we observe in medicine, law, business, and academia. We see it in athletics at earlier and earlier ages.

The second characteristic is the speed at which we live our lives. Look around. Most people are impatient and seem to grow more so as technology accelerates the way we get things done.

Characteristic number three is the attraction for short-cuts, or the universal willingness to accept the shallow or the superficial, adopting a path simply because it is easy rather than demanding.

The question Porter asked was, "How do we feel about our constant need for bigger, better, and faster in our pursuit of excellence?"

In answering that question, he asked his audience to step back several centuries in time to another day, as we try and make sense of the best way to deal with our "today." The place is Greece, the time is about 300 years B.C. and the concept is excellence.

The Greek word *arête`* that Dr. Porter referred to is perhaps the most articulated value in Greek culture, because it is the ultimate definition of excellence. Aristotle referred to *arête`* as virtue. Virtue in Aristotle's culture held a vastly different meaning than it does today. Its essence is the sum of all the corporeal or mental excellences, such as strength, vigor, bravery, courage, aptness, capability, worth, wisdom, piety, endurance, self-control, and goodness. With this as the perspective, notice how the word *excellence* takes on a depth, a breadth, and even a richness that isn't found in the way we use the same word today.

With an eye toward the Greek definition of excellence, let's consider a second dimension of *arête* as the concept of great effort and striving—of doing one's best. This does not require defeating or prevailing over others. It is essentially being and doing one's absolute best—becoming the best person one can become. Considering that high ideal, isn't it sad that our need to "win" often overshadows the virtue of doing our very best?

Arête is not about winning, or competition, or a quest for superiority. It is about intellectual, physical, and spiritual excellence. Its characteristics could be demonstrated in competition such as the games made famous by the ancient Greeks. But complete excellence of person is not found in one's ability to win.

The pursuit of excellence recognizes that true excellence requires much effort, time and improvement of character. Success does not come instantly or quickly; it is the product of a lifetime of planning, striving, failing, and achieving.

Theodore Roosevelt summarized it pretty well when he said: "The credit belongs to the man who is actually in the arena, whose face is marred by dust and sweat and blood, who strives valiantly, who errs and comes up short again and again, because there is no effort without error or shortcoming, but who knows the great enthusiasms, the great devotions, who spends himself for a worthy cause; who, at the best, knows, in the end, the triumph of high achievement, and who, at the worst, if he fails, at least he fails while daring greatly, so that his place shall never be with those timid souls who knew neither victory nor defeat."[10]

The Excellence Culture

We sought excellence of person, mind, and character in the people we hired. Such principles of excellence helped them change the way they viewed their work and the results they were trying to accomplish.

In our quest to instill excellence into the hearts and minds of our associates, we also taught the value of self-determination. We did so by teaching the liberating principle that they were their own boss; they were the entrepreneurs; they were the owners of their own businesses. Even though we provided them with office services, ongoing education, training, and consultation on important cases, the people we hired were still in charge of their own individual business entity.

We taught them that they were in charge of themselves. The core of that process was based on a question: "Do you know what you must do to be successful?" No matter what the answer was, we taught them a new core affirmation that we believed in: "I do what I do because I believe in quality."

Because they believed in producing quality, it was relatively easy for them to buy into the concept that they were the boss. In that process, they began to act and think of themselves as employers, rather than as employees. As they completed this personal metamorphosis, they became more aware of the opportunities and obstacles before them. And as they did so, the quality of their lives and their economic well-being improved dramatically.

If you are a longstanding NCAA football fanatic, do you

remember the glory days of LaVell Edwards's BYU football teams? From the late seventies through the nineties, excellence was the hallmark of those teams. Some of the best, record-setting quarterbacks in NCAA history, along with many future great NFL players came out of that program. Edward's coaching record is legendary. On the day he retired, among active coaches he was ranked third in number of wins, behind Joe Paterno and Bobby Bowden. His teams were always highly ranked; they even won the national championship in 1984.

But that was then and this is now. Edwards retired, things changed and the BYU football program went into sort of a cruise-control mode. But the next three years were disappointing. During the Edwards era, BYU football had never before experienced three losing seasons in a row, but for all kinds of reasons those next three seasons were painful, losing seasons, and moments of excellence were rare.

So when BYU defensive coordinator, Bronco Mendenhall, was handed the head-coaching job in December 2004, it came with a mandate that reached well beyond winning football games. He took upon himself the unenviable task of rebuilding a once proud football program, and returning it to its previous prominent position. Speaking on behalf of the team in his first press conference, he said: "I think we're the flag bearer of this school. I intend to carry that flag up high—not on the ground. If I do my job right, this place will be one of the most dominant programs in the country, as it once was."[11]

This was heady stuff, and for a new head football coach who was only in his thirties and had no prior head-coaching experience, Mendenhall's predictions were very bold, particularly as he was taking over a losing program.

But Mendenhall was serious. He had a vision and an uncompromising spirit. He actually believed that if his players could buy in to his philosophy and work ethic, which included the development of the whole-man concept, they could accomplish every goal. In the process, they would develop into men of true greatness and integrity.

Early on, there were some in the press who mocked Mendenhall's plans to return the BYU football to a position of national prominence. How could he actually say those things out loud? Shouldn't he just keep that to himself?

Well, he didn't keep those things to himself. Players who couldn't accept the rigors of his new program left the team. Others, who didn't leave because they only had a year to go to graduate, kind of hung around and privately bad-mouthed the program. After all, this new coach was requiring harder work and accountability—outrageous!

In addition to that, there were lots of other detractors, particularly when the team started off the 2005 season by losing three games and winning only one. By season's end, the team had won six games and lost five. And then, in their first bowl game in four years, they lost thirty-five to twenty-eight in a "heartbreaker" against Cal, Berkeley.

Mendenhall's first season was somewhat disappointing to the impatient football fan. But the fans were in for a surprise. At that stage, little did they know about the heart and mind of Bronco Mendenhall and his new team of totally committed, focused young men.

In the winter 2007 edition of the *BYU Magazine*, there was an article about the Mendenhall excellence paradigm; Associate Editor Peter Gardner summarized the process of returning this once-great program to its former position of national prominence:

"Right away, Mendenhall set out three principles that he felt needed immediate attention—accountability, discipline, and effort. He wanted players who would do what they said they were going to do at a level that demonstrated precision and discipline ..."[11]

As smart as Mendenhall is, he realized that he is not the fountain of all knowledge. So when someone suggested that Business Management Consultant Paul Gustavson give him ideas to spread his vision throughout his team, Mendenhall made the call ... "Gustavson emphasized that to compete successfully, an organization cannot be just like its competition. The principle meshed with Mendenhall's developing vision of BYU football.

He also stressed that 'all organizations are perfectly designed to get the results they get.' BYU's most recent results were three losing seasons and a handful of off-field problems. So if Mendenhall wanted penetrating change, Gustavson insisted, he couldn't just add a fresh coat of paint to the same structure ...

Mendenhall learned on day one that not everyone would welcome his brand of intensity. Even before the first team meeting, a player showed up in suit and tie at Mendenhall's office and said, 'This program is not for me.'

When Mendenhall asked why, the player responded, 'I know what you're going to expect, and I'm not willing to do that.'

Two more players quit the next day ...

To describe why one player quits and another thrives,

Mendenhall refers to a commitment scale he discovered in his management readings. At one end are those who rebel or quit. Next are the players who do what is asked, but only out of 'malicious obedience.' At the other end of the spectrum are players who act out of 'heartfelt commitment' and 'creative enthusiasm.' While most players still stand somewhere in the middle, Mendenhall says the commitment level has risen dramatically ..."11

Not only has the level of commitment from existing team members risen, so has the level of recruiting. The surprise is that the coaching staff does not go into the homes of prospective recruits and sugarcoat the rigors of being a member of BYU's team. To the contrary, those recruiters completely divulge their expectations for full dedication and commitment, not only to unbelievably hard work ethics, but also to the strictest student honor code in the NCAA.

"One might think that with so many demands on players, BYU's recruiting pool would be too small to be competitive. While the options are limited, Mendenhall has found the high standards to be more of a help than a hindrance. They're coming now because of these things. It can be used as a competitive advantage."11

There is much more that could be said about the Bronco Mendenhall way of building a winning football program, while simultaneously building young men, but it seems sufficient to say that his second, third, and subsequent seasons as head coach produced similar winning records and culminated in winning back-to-back bowl games for the first time in eleven years.

If you were thinking that this story was about college

football, you'd be wrong. It was about excellence, commitment, and leadership, and how such thinking changes results in organizations and people. It was about Albert E.N. Gray's timeless message: "The common denominator of success—the secret of success of every man who has ever been successful—lies in the fact that he formed the habit of doing things that failures don't like to do."

Here's the lesson:

- Success requires specialization and living up to one's full potential.
- Success does not come instantly or quickly, but is the product of a lifetime.
- I do what I do because I believe in quality.
- Success requires attention to accountability, discipline, and effort.

Chapter Seven

Quality Leadership Equals Quality Results

*Quality is never an accident; it is always the result of high
intention, sincere effort, intelligent direction, and skillful
execution; it represents the wise choice of many alternatives.*

—Willa A. Foster

I have always been driven by the need to do better. I didn't
always succeed, but in the trying, I was able to accomplish
things that I would never have accomplished if I had been shy
about getting on with it. Those who know me well know that
I believe, as I said earlier, that "the secret to getting something
done is to do it now." Such an attitude has served me well over
the years, and while a few might have criticized my zealous
nature, most were grateful to be part of a personal philosophy
that gave no fellowship to procrastination.

In our agency, total quality meant many things, including
the ability to get and stay focused. From their first day of basic
training, we taught our new people to concentrate on things
that were within their control, so that they could maximize
their energy output toward those things. Conversely, we
taught that if they wasted energy trying to work on the things

that they could not control, they would never quite reach their potential.

Some years ago, I hired a very sharp young man, who came highly recommended. Our interviews and the results of his aptitude tests indicated that he would be a total winner. As he made his way through his basic training, he completed all assignments and every task. We found him to be one of the brightest in the class. However, this trainee did not live up to his potential. Early in his career he was relatively successful, but as the months went by, his activity, and consequently his production, began to lag. I inquired about the problem and found that he was working part-time as a building contractor in order to make ends meet.

I told him that we didn't have any part-time people working for us. First, because there was no way for him to stay focused on all the things that were required in our educational process, and second, because our organization was dedicated to total professionalism. For him to try and divide his time and energy between two totally unrelated disciplines was not only an impossible task, but it was unacceptable. He couldn't understand. He had a couple of friends who were new in the business, working for another company, and they were working part-time.

I asked him if he would ever go to a part-time doctor for a check-up, let alone surgery. I asked if he would ever go to a part-time dentist for a check-up, let alone a root canal. When he said he would not, I asked how he could expect a client to be happy with a part-time financial advisor who would be making recommendations which would profoundly affect the client's long or short-term financial security.

He said that he could see the point, but his plan was to just do this construction work until he was back on his feet financially. I told him that it was impossible to "serve two masters," and that if he could not commit one hundred percent of his time to the development of his career, we couldn't allow him to be part of our organization.

Financial problems had little to do with our trainee's difficulties in getting his new career under way. The real issues were his personal discipline and his lack of commitment to a values system that required him to learn everything necessary to take care of his clients' financial needs. With this attitude, there was no way that our recruit would be able to provide the quality and service that our clientele had come to expect from us.

My sharp, high-aptitude young recruit had displayed many outward gifts that indicated a propensity for total success. But what we could not measure, in spite of having one of the best recruiting procedures in the industry, was his heart and his ability to see the need for total quality for every client. He could not see that his lack of commitment to the development of his career affected not only him and his financial requirements, but it also affected his ability to provide his clients with the best financial advice and consultation available. In the final analysis, his real problem was that he could not see that this was a career. He thought it was just a job.

Total Quality

Steven Covey, the business consulting guru, said: "Total quality is an expression of the need for continuous improvement in four areas: (1) personal and professional development, (2) interpersonal relations, (3) managerial effectiveness, and (4) organizational productivity."[12]

These four areas required improvement not only from those who were leading our organization, but also from all of our associates who actually believed that they were in charge of their own business interests within the organization. As we built our young organization, this is the perspective we believed in, and these are the principles we constantly tried to instill in our people.

As a result, much of what we did as we planned and built our agency was based on this principle-centered approach to leadership. We learned this approach over many years of studying Covey's insights on the factors that make organizations and people successful.

Let's consider the need for continuous improvement in each of the four areas mentioned earlier.

Personal and Professional Development

We learned that character and skill development is an ongoing process that requires progression and measured improvement. It becomes a continual upward spiral. We tried to instill the belief that the personal side of total quality meant total integrity around each person's system of values, and part of that system meant that they were always striving to improve, both personally and professionally. Those who were willing to reach for such results found themselves among the few that became totally referable.

However, a great deal of sacrifice may be necessary if one is to be classed among the great, and since the resulting pain doesn't come naturally, few are willing to pay this price. Yet, we insisted on constancy of purpose, a principle which we taught our new recruits, and which focuses on what we can become if we are prepared to be dedicated and fully committed to our goals.

Interpersonal Relations

Total quality at this level requires regular deposits into what my friend Steven Covey calls the emotional bank account.[8] Such deposits are created by continually building goodwill and negotiating with others in good faith, but never in fear. Creating expectations of continuous product or service improvement, but then failing to deliver, will only build up fear and negative forecasting from previous and potential customers. When that happens, we not only become "nonreferable," but the ensuing bad-mouthing that a frustrated customer initiates can kill a potential market.

Managerial Effectiveness

Our most effective management tool is win-win thinking, which creates interfunctional teamwork where everyone buys into the value of others' individual contributions, even though everyone's assignment is different. But in the process, we had to be careful to steer clear of win-lose egocentric thinking, which could only have created interfunctional rivalry. "Rivalries," in Covey's words, "are very natural when people have limited resources; they perceive their professional world as a limited pie, and gradually develop win-lose approaches. They sit and talk about 'those guys' over there and about what they are going to do to build their personal empires. Win-lose competition is fueled by bad-mouthing other people behind their backs. Our fiercest competitors are then right inside our own divisions or departments."

By learning that concept early in the development of our top-quality organization, we were able to break away from what was typical with the big crowd of average agencies in the industry.

By working *within* established systems, effective management practices require a different way of looking at problems and potential solutions. Leadership, on the other hand, works *to change* those systems; it deals with direction, vision, purpose, and principles. As a result, it builds people, culture, and relationships. Management deals more with control, logistics, and efficiency. It deals with the bottom line, whereas leadership deals with the top line. Having said that, it is necessary that both leadership and management be effective and efficient.

Organizational Productivity

Proactive leadership grows from an awareness that we are not products of systems or environments. It's true that those things influence us greatly, but we can choose our response to them. Being proactive is the essence of effective leadership. All great leaders have a very high level of proactive energy— that energy that comes from within and is not dependent upon the energy of others. Such energy provides vision and a sense that "I am not a product of my culture, my conditioning, and the conditions of my life; rather, I am a product of my principles, values, attitudes, beliefs, and behavior. Those things I control."[8]

In the early days, we didn't know much about how to become a great organization. Today, we know significantly more, and we have learned that quality starts at the top. The leadership of the organization must be intimately involved in the process to see that this quality perspective is instilled into the minds and hearts of everybody in the organization. What we've learned is a more principle-centered approach to life and leadership.

We enhanced that principle-centered approach to agency building by being fully engaged and committed to the success of each individual associate.

The Power of Full Engangemnt

The Power of Full Engagement is a great book by Jim Loehr, one of the nation's most renowned psychologists, who is the head of LGE Performance Systems in Orlando. Jim spent more than twenty-five years learning what makes people successful. He wanted to know what made people perform at their peak level, whether it was in sports, in business, or in life. Working with a wide range of people, from top athletes, Fortune 500 executives, top-government employees, to homemakers or stay-at-home moms, Loehr reached powerful conclusions; he suggests that these conclusions will change the way we think about what we want from life, and how we are going to get it. Thanks to an interview that he did with Ken McAlpine for the February 2003 issue of *Southwest Spirit,* we have the following potpourri of thoughts, which are detailed in his book. Consider his recommendations below and see if their application in your particular situation will make a difference.

"We have more demands on our time and energy than

we've ever seen in our history. [Our approach] is about helping people understand how they can train and mobilize their resources so that they can complete whatever mission they're on, without sacrificing their health and happiness.

The notion of full engagement in what you do is the most critical element in being able to complete any kind of mission you're on. It's not just mental and physical toughness, it's also physical and spiritual. In order to be fully engaged you have to be physically energized, emotionally connected, mentally focused, and spiritually aligned with whatever the mission is.

You have to be emotionally connected to what's going on, you have to be there, fully present emotionally, and in a very positive way. If you're negative, angry, upset, nervous, or afraid, those emotions tend to lock you up (as opposed to the sense of adventure, the sense of challenge and opportunity). Then you have to be mentally focused. Concentration is simply focused energy. If you're not focused mentally, with your attention directed at the most important, relevant parts of a challenging situation, you have virtually no chance of summoning your talent and being your best. We find ways to multitask, to be kind of half there. What multitasking means is you're not fully engaged."[13]

When we were focused and fully engaged we consistently instilled the principle of top quality into the hearts of each associate. Gaining top quality from every associate required us to recruit and retain individuals who had personal attributes that rendered them receptive to top-quality thinking and results. We had a very impressive record of recruiting and retaining such individuals. We were continually among the leading agencies in the company and were ranked the number one agency ten times, and we ranked second or third every other year for twenty-six years. As much as I joked about it when outsiders would ask how we did that—to which I would respond that it was nothing more than "pure dumb luck"—I knew, in fact, that it was just the opposite. I knew that the road we had taken to accomplish our lofty goals and dreams was very different than the road that most of our competition had chosen.

Our continuing affirmation of the basic principles of total quality was an integral part of the roadmap that made us one of the best agencies in our business. The difference that those principles made in the lives and careers of our associates is remarkable. We weren't just lucky.

If you use these principles along with Emerson's timeless statement on persistence within the common denominator framework of success, you will have the foundation pieces necessary to accomplish greater results than ever before.

Here's the lesson:

- The secret to getting something done is to do it now.
- Until new recruits view their work as a career, they will see it as "just a job."
- Total quality requires continuous improvement.
- To be fully engaged, you must be physically energized, emotionally connected, mentally focused, and spiritually aligned with the mission.

Chapter Eight

We're Looking for a Few Good Men

I'm convinced that ours is not a career for ordinary people. It takes a person with guts, determination, ambition, desire, and plenty of old-fashioned virtue to weather the storms of this business.

— Lyle Blessman

Like the Marine Corp. we were constantly looking for just a few good men and women who fit our mold of the associate we sought. As I said in the last chapter, the individual we sought, in our rather narrow recruiting approach, was a self-starter, self-motivator, self-disciplinarian, who could go easily to people. Applicants who lacked any one of those four characteristics wouldn't make it in our business. Knowing what I know about sales organizations, I dare say that anybody who intends to be successful in selling anything must have these four characteristics, or they will not be successful over time.

During the years that we were building these successful life insurance agencies, the average life insurance company had a first-year retention rate of 20 percent. By the end of the second year, only 10 percent of the people who had been hired in the first year were still in the business.

I wish I could tell you that everybody we hired stayed in the business and made it a career. They didn't. But compared to industry results, we did a pretty good job. On the average, during three decades of agency-building in California and Utah, our first-year retention rate was 60 percent. At the end of the second year, our rate of retention was 40 percent. We did a study of our retention rate for the history of our Utah agency, and found that after nineteen years, 24 percent of the people we hired were still with the company. We felt pretty good about that. We got the results we got because we planned it that way. As my management team and I matured, we came to the determination that ours would be an organization of dedicated, professional, honorable individuals who would lead the company in production. The only way that could happen was if we provided them with a roadmap and a compass, as it were, that would help them get from where they were to where they wanted to be.

We did that in several ways. First, as I said earlier, we taught our people to think and act as if they owned the place. We wanted strong, independent people who would be in business to stay. We appealed to their entrepreneurial nature; we also provided an office environment that included furniture, computers, executive assistance, and back-room technology that they couldn't get if they left us and went to any other company.

Second, my sales managers and I knew how to sell, and our agents knew it. They knew that not only could we help them design the case in such a way that it would sell, but they also knew that we would go with them, when necessary, to close the case, and that when the sale happened, we would not take any of the commission—it would all be theirs. You can imagine the loyalty that bought.

When other managers learned of our approach to building relationships with our associates that stayed glued, they were often incredulous to think that we would not take part of the commission. We were willing to do that, because it demonstrated our commitment to being the "value added" to our organization. It was one of the factors that bought the loyalty and gained the retention results we had obtained over all those years. When I tried to explain this approach and the loyalty that it bought, some managers said, "I could never do that."

I said: "You can do it if you want to, but if you continue to do what you've always done, you'll continue to get what you've always got."

Third, there were countless little things we did that made up our leadership and management style. For example, unless I had a breakfast appointment with an agent or a client, I usually got to the office between 7:30 and 8:00 a.m. I usually did not leave the office until 6:00 p.m., unless one of my kids was involved in a little league or a high school game. That kind of personal discipline and example on our part did not go unnoticed. The winners in our organization began to arrive a little earlier and stay a little later, because that's what they saw us doing. The "good" people we were seeking responded positively to the example we were setting; they would emulate it and pass it on to others. What everyone began to see was that it's incredible what you can do with that extra hour on each end of the work day.

My management team and I weren't workaholics, but we were focused, calendared, and scheduled. I often took Friday off, and I vacationed in Hawaii two or three times a year. I never missed a game, a play, a recital, a birthday, or an anniversary. When I worked, I really worked. When it was time to play, I really played.

The fourth thing we taught our people was that when they're feeling a little stressed out or finding it hard to get organized, they should simply stand (rather than sit) at their desk, and get on with the day's activities and phone calls. I'm serious. I got so much done on the stress-filled days by simply standing and walking around the office while I talked on the phone, filed, checked on items, and even had short management meetings.

You may be saying, "That's all well and good, but the fact is I'm so busy, I don't seem to get it all done every day, no matter what time I arrive at the office." If that's true, you may find some value in considering the way I approached organizing my office so that everything had a place and was easily retrievable.

In your experience every day, there are constant interruptions; someone knocks on your door, your phone rings or an unscheduled meeting has been called and you have to be there. The important things are constantly being pushed aside for whatever appears to be the most urgent and pressing. There is too much to do and not enough hours in the day.

The simple solution is to get organized, and the place to

start is right at your desk. First of all, set aside two hours of totally uninterrupted time. That doesn't work very well unless you're willing to close the door, tell your executive assistant that there will be absolutely no phone calls, and then get prepared to throw things away.

Start with any stacks on your desk, go through every piece of paper, and ask yourself three really important questions:

- What is this?
- Why do I have this?
- What am I supposed to do with it?

If you can't come up with great answers, then chuck it! When that's complete, start going through every file or folder in your desk and do the very same thing. You'll discover that a huge percentage of what's in those files can be thrown out.

As you sort through everything, make a stack with everything in it that you intend to keep. As you go through that stack, make a priority list of every piece of paper. After the list is complete, make sure that you have listed the most important things in a *first-things-first* order, to prioritize that list immediately.

If you don't already have a great filing system set up, both alphabetically and topically, fix that now. Doing so relieves you of expending emotional energy, searching for stuff that should be immediately available to you, but isn't.

Make it a habit to keep all related papers, documents, and information on your clients together in their own individual file. Having two or more files on the same client promises distraction and disorganization. Date every document and piece of paper that you put into its file, and don't put unfinished work into a file without identifying that task on your priority list.

Sounds simple, doesn't it? It is. Follow this scenario and unclutter your life. When you do, you'll find a new freedom that gives you more physical and emotional energy to deal with the things that matter most, when they matter most.

Personal organization is one of the key elements in leading your organization by example. As you do that, you maximize your mental and emotional energy.

Here's a final list of management concepts that I used in conducting business. Hopefully, these suggestions will give new meaning to the work you do and the way you do it.

- Stop comparing yourself to others. Compare yourself to you. You do that by simply saying: "Would I be proud to show this to anyone else?"

- Avoid quick judgments. It's got to be an awfully thin piece of paper that only has one side.

- Be a light to all your associates. It will bring great strength to the organization.

- Develop your own mission statement and live by it.

- You cannot vary from the plan, even when you just don't have the energy to face an issue. Make your honor greater than your moods.

- If you don't have a burning need to make a difference, you're in the wrong business. Get out.

- Learn to separate the urgent from the important and then follow through on those things in priority order.

- Remember that even if you're on the right track, you'll get run over if you just stand there.

Over the twenty-eight years that I was building agencies in the insurance industry, we were very fortunate to have hired top-quality people who did not embarrass or disappoint us because of illegal or unethical practices. However, there was one individual who was different. He tested well; he interviewed well. When we checked his references, everyone gave him high praise. He was a quick learner and a very hard worker. He only had one flaw. He was dishonest, and we didn't know it. By that I mean that he would sometimes exaggerate or fail to disclose certain information which, if it had been disclosed, might have caused the client not to buy.

Because he was young in the business, I initially chalked it up to inexperience and his failure to understand the mission statement about how we treat the client.

These problems with him didn't happen all the time, but when they did, it was usually in connection with a substantial case. When the client would complain, I would be notified and immediately arrange to meet with him and the agent together, learn what the problem was, clarify what should have been explained, and offer to direct the company to return all money paid, if necessary. Usually, the clarifying explanation was acceptable and the client left happy, because he now knew exactly what to plan for. I would correct and "school" the agent on his mistake, and things would settle back down to normal.

However, as time went by, the complaints increased. I would make apologies to the client, and he would leave happy, or he would, at least, leave satisfied, because he got his money back.

We finally realized that we couldn't afford to have this agent represent us any longer. Our reputation was too hard-won to allow this man, who was suffering from delusions of greatness, to destroy what had taken years to build. Even though he had become our biggest producer, we terminated his contract and notified all of his clients that he was no longer with us.

In your quest to find the kind of people we sought, be very careful of those who view your mission statement and your culture with impudence. When their way doesn't line up with your way, get rid of them in a hurry. You'll save a lot of heartache, criticism, and money.

Here's the lesson:

- The new associates you seek must be self-starters, self-motivators, self-disciplinarians and can go easily to people.
- Unclutter your life and your desk, and you'll find a new freedom that gives you more physical and emotional energy.
- If you don't have a burning desire to make a difference, you are in the wrong part of the business.
- Be very careful of those who treat your mission statement and your culture with impudence.

Chapter Nine

I Love Knowledge

An educated man is not one whose memory is trained to carry a few dates in history. He is one who can accomplish things. A man who cannot think is not an educated man, however many college degrees he may have acquired. Thinking is the hardest work anyone can do, which is probably the reason why we have so few thinkers.

—Henry Ford

My father, who brought me into the business of insurance and financial services in 1966, was the smartest man I ever met. He was exceptional. Eventually, my two younger brothers and my brother-in-law came into the business as well. When Dad was sixty-five, he finally retired from the business, and turned most of his clients over to his sons.

As a new retiree, he spent a lot of time involved in volunteer work. Occasionally one of his bigger clients would call him, asking for special help on a particular case, but though he responded to their requests, he stopped spending time, every day, developing new client relationships like he did before retiring.

As a result, you can imagine my surprise to learn that, at

age seventy-one, my father was pursuing a master's degree in financial science. I couldn't believe it.

I called him and said, "Dad, I just found out that you are working on a master's degree in financial science."

He said, "Yes, I am."

"What on earth could that possibly do for you at this stage in life? Why are you doing this?"

He answered: "I love knowledge."

Wow! I could hardly wait to share that with every one of my associates. What a fabulous thing for Dad to say, and what a great thing for me to spotlight, as the manager of dozens of younger associates, some of whom were dragging their feet at the educational requirements outlined for our organization. If this seventy-one-year-old manager was continuing to expand his knowledge, if retirement hadn't dampened his desire to further understand our business's complexities, how could any of our young agents claim that more education wasn't "all that important?" They were impressed, and we were able to use my dad's quest for knowledge as the example for their pursuit of excellence through our industry's continuing education programs.

In an earlier chapter, we talked about the debilitating effects of fear. The key to overcoming fear is knowledge. Our persistent pursuit of knowledge was one of the keys to our success. We had this constant need to learn everything possible about what successful people did. The more we learned, the more courage we gained. Increased knowledge brought more courage. Have you not seen it in your own life?

One of the reasons we were among the best agency-builders in the business was because of our belief in ongoing education about our industry, its products, our competitors, tax law, accounting, investments, and economic issues. The more knowledgeable our people were about that, as well as estate-planning problems and what makes business work, the more courageous they were about approaching those whose financial situations required a review of those problems. We learned that the key to success in any endeavor is knowledge. Knowledge is king, and when we applied our quest for knowledge to our products and relevant parts of the Internal Revenue Code, we obtained the success we sought.

We were always reading everything we could get our hands on about what was going on in our business. We attended every local, state, or national conference that was available to us. We invited the best in our business to teach us in our own agency. If they couldn't come to us, we went to them. We learned what the best in our industry were doing and emulated it. We learned, first-hand, the absolute truth of Emerson's great statement, and "that which we persisted in doing" about the educational pursuits of our agency actually became easier for us to do.

Kim Clark, the former Dean of Harvard's Business School, recently gave a talk, titled "Learning is the Key" to a national management society. In it, he outlined several principles of business success that he had discovered in his professional career. He said: "Two plants for the same company, with exactly the same product, the same customers, and the same market will perform differently. There is no explanation, no theory to explain the variants, but they are there. The key is that companies and individuals who have the capacity to learn will have significant advantage in the competitive world. Learning is absolutely vital to a company's success.

If you look around, companies that have sustained success over time are really good at learning. They exploit existing variants, and learn, and become more effective.

If you, as a leader, can teach people in your organization why you are doing certain things so that they come to internalize those values, you will find this approach to be very powerful. It will enable you to move people to do amazing things.

Successful organizations have figured out how to tap the potential that is in human beings. It is remarkable what people will do when they work in an organization where leaders create meaning, have integrity, care about the worker [and provide them with knowledge about how things really are.]"[14]

Learning and the ongoing acquisition of knowledge at every level of the company is one of the keys to building and maintaining great organizations. Managers who have learned that are able to lead their companies to sustained growth and improvement every year. Those who have not, are relegated to repeating past mistakes and spending a lot of time correcting and redefining problems. In the process, they never accomplish the great things that could have been accomplished had they actively pursued knowledge.

Dad's love of knowledge was a classic illustration that learning is the key to understanding things as they really are.

It may be that you are sitting there saying, "I think I'm in trouble. I've been climbing this proverbial ladder of success, but I can now see that my ladder has been leaning against the wrong wall."

Maybe you're saying, "I don't really have to do all those things, do I?"

No, you really don't. It's your call. But remember that if you continue to do things the way you've always done them, the results will be about the same as before. Remember, too, that if you are unprepared for the opportunities that come, those opportunities will slip through your fingers like sand. Nothing prepares us better for opportunities than the acquisition and application of knowledge.

Because of knowledge our people were the best-prepared financial advisors in the business. Consequently, their clients were better served, while other members of the client's financial advisory team—including their attorneys and their accountants—found our advisors' work to be both professional and unique.

As a result, our associates' referrals came from both the client and his advisors, which ultimately opened certain doors to those advisors. It was one of the reasons why we received the Master Agency Builder Award in 1983, which recognized us as being among the top 100 agencies in the country. We were grateful for the recognition, but we were even more grateful to have determined associates who were committed to obtaining the knowledge that made them totally professional and the best at what they did.

Pat Riley summarized it this way: "When you meet a challenge *fully prepared*, your effort flows seamlessly. There is concentration and exertion, but no straining. When you go after a goal and you're not prepared, you soon find yourself pressing. The harder you try the less effective you become. The less effective [you are], the more discouraged [you get]—

until finally you have an iron-clad conviction that you will fail. Poor preparation is an enemy of free-breathing performance and an invitation to choking."

Notice how Riley's profound statement meshes with Shakespeare's *Julius Caesar.* A classic line from that play sums up the meaning of being prepared for the opportunities we seek: "There is a tide in the affairs of men which taken at the flood, leads on to fortune. Omitted, all the voyage of their lives is bound in shallows and in misery. On such a full sea are we now afloat and we must take the current when it serves, or lose our ventures."

That full sea is the acquisition of knowledge. The practical application of it is vital to the accomplishment of great things in your business.

Here's the lesson:

- Companies that have sustained success, over time, have valued and promoted learning.
- It is remarkable what people will do when they work in an organization where leaders create meaning.
- Learning and the ongoing acquisition of knowledge are two of the keys to building and maintaining a great company.
- When you are fully prepared to meet a challenge, your effort flows seamlessly.

Chapter Ten

The Power Of Discipline

If you could kick the person responsible for most of your troubles,
you wouldn't be able to sit down for six months.

—Gordon Gray

One of the most troubling problems in America today is a general lack of personal discipline. This phenomenon, evident in people of all ages, can be closely linked to the financial crisis this country has undergone over the last few years. It's been an agonizing time. Almost everything in our financial markets has been in commotion. The violent swings we have witnessed in market value have been fearful. Along with this commotion and fear comes a culture which promotes less accountability, more leisure, more entertainment, more welfare, less self-control, and less personal responsibility. All of these things have created a general lack of trust and discipline in the lives of so many, and a frightening drift away from excellence in individual lives and business. Consequently, those of us who grew up with a mind-set that "you can accomplish anything you want to accomplish, as long as you're willing to pay the price for it," often have a difficult time convincing younger people that the "Law of the Harvest" is a never-changing principle that cannot be circumvented if one hopes to attain his goals and dreams.

That Law is as simple as it sounds. The law of the harvest simply means that there are absolutes that never change, and that these must be followed if one intends to accomplish objectives.

In farming, the objective is a fall harvest that produces the right quantity and the right quality of produce, ready for market, which will bring the right price. None of that will happen unless a series of other events happen exactly on time, and in order, every single year. Everything that happens in the life of the farmer, from obtaining an operating loan, to spring-plowing the land on time, to harrowing the land, to planting seeds, to irrigating, to weeding, thinning, and spraying the crop, all bring the desired result at harvest time in the fall.

Few farmers indulge in "goofing off" or questioning whether or not they feel like doing the job of the day. They know that eliminating or delaying even one step of the production process impacts the harvest and may jeopardize their financial future. As a result, they learn personal discipline at a young age and teach it to their children. Farmers get what they get because they plan it that way.

The law of the harvest applies in business as well. If we discipline ourselves to plan, focus, and follow through, the results will be as planned—as long as the plan is realistic and bullet-proof. Even though plans do not remain bullet-proof over time (they are subject to market forces and an ever-changing global economy), the successful business owner utilizes his experience to make his plan as bullet-proof as possible.

The undisciplined among us rarely plan, rarely focus, and rarely follow through; they get paid accordingly. They are continually disappointed in life because their acceptance of mediocrity and their undisciplined, "I don't like to be told what to do" mentality, kills their understanding of the law of the harvest.

Jim Collins's book, *Good to Great*, cuts through all the "red tape" of success in business and gets right to the heart of the matter, disproving that you have to be superhuman to accomplish lofty and worthy goals.

In the book, we learn the story of George Rathmann and the 1980 founding of his biotechnology company, Amgen. "Over the next twenty years, Amgen grew from a struggling entrepreneurial enterprise, into a $3.2 billion company with 6,400 employees, creating blood products to improve the lives of people suffering from the effects of chemotherapy and kidney dialysis. Under Rathman, Amgen became one of the few biotechnology companies that delivered consistent profitability and growth. In fact it became so consistently profitable that its stock price multiplied over 150 times from its public offering in June 1983 to January 2000."[15]

Of all the great leadership principles, none is more essential to the success of a business venture than that which favors mature simplicity over unnecessary sophistication. Mature simplicity requires personal discipline and that is why so many men and women never arrive at that place in their business lives.

In chapter 6 of *Good to Great*, Collins wrote:

"Few successful start-ups become great companies, in large part because they respond to growth and success in the wrong way. Entrepreneurial success is fueled by creativity, imagination, bold moves into uncharted waters, and visionary zeal. As a company grows and becomes more complex, it begins to trip over its own success—too many new people, too many new customers, too many new orders, too many new products. What was once great fun becomes an unwieldy ball of disorganized stuff. Lack of planning, lack of accounting, lack of systems, and lack of hiring constraints create friction. Problems surface—with customers, with cash flow, with schedules.

In response, someone (often a board member) says, 'It's time to grow up. This place needs some professional management.' The company begins to hire MBAs and seasoned executives from blue-chip companies. Processes, procedures, checklists, and all the rest begin to sprout up like weeds. What was once an egalitarian environment gets replaced with a hierarchy. Chains of command appear for the first time. Reporting relationships become clear, and an executive class with special perks begins to appear. 'We' and 'they' segmentations appear— just like in a real company. The professional managers finally rein in the mess. They create order out of chaos, but they also kill the entrepreneurial spirit. Members of the founding team begin to grumble, 'This isn't fun anymore. I used to be able to get things done. Now I have to fill out these stupid forms and follow these stupid rules. Worst of all, I have to spend a horrendous amount of time in meetings.' The creative magic begins to wane as some of the most innovative people leave, disgusted by the burgeoning bureaucracy and hierarchy. The exciting start-up transforms itself into just another company, with nothing special to recommend it. The cancer of mediocrity begins to grow in earnest."[15]

Both big and little business ventures thrive on mature simplicity. The leaders of those companies thrive on it because they expect the business plan to succeed, and they know that without mature simplicity, the chance of failure increases. Just as the bureaucracy described above ends up stumbling over its own unnecessary sophistication, so, too, will the smallest business venture get bogged down if the right people are not in place and filling the roles they are most qualified to fill. Planning and executing all business plans is done successfully if those who lead adopt the maturely simple way.

"George Rathmann avoided this entrepreneurial death spiral. He understood that the purpose of bureaucracy is to compensate for incompetence and lack of discipline—a problem that largely goes away if you have the right people in the first place. Most companies build their bureaucratic rules to manage the small percentage of wrong people on the bus, which in turn drives away the right people on the bus, which then increases the percentage of wrong people on the bus, which increases the need for more bureaucracy to compensate for incompetence and lack of discipline, which then further drives the right people away ..."[15]

We learned that it takes discipline to "stay the course," as Rathmann did, but in our agency, we did this while regularly honing and refining our system of putting the "right people on the bus," and getting the "wrong people" off the bus. Implementing this strategy enabled us to "purify" the culture and eliminate the emotional energy and unnecessary expense of dealing with "wrong people." We found, early on, that holding on to wrong people undermined our mission. We were determined to keep the right people on the bus.

In his research, on the *good-to-great* companies, Collins was amazed to find the constant use of words like disciplined, rigorous, determined, diligent, precise, systematic, methodical, demanding, consistent, focused, accountable, and responsible. But he found that those words were not in the materials on the direct comparison companies. The companies in *Good-to-Great* "became somewhat more extreme in the fulfillment of their responsibilities, bordering in some cases on fanaticism."[17]

As a young, tentative new manager for my company, I had no idea what made the great organizations great. But I began to get a clearer picture from relatively small but significant lessons, found in such unlikely places as picture captions. If you recall, in Chapter Two I mentioned the caption below the picture of the peacock: "How glorious it is, and also how painful, to be an exception." It's true that I had a lot yet to learn in those days, but over the years, my own personal experience in both athletics and business, taught me that striving for excellence is both glorious and painful.

Here's the lesson:

- Attaining goals and dreams requires adhering to the law of the harvest.
- The undisciplined rarely plan, rarely focus, rarely follow through, and they get paid accordingly.
- Avoid complicated sophistication and embrace mature simplicity.
- Get the wrong people off the bus and the right people on the bus.

Chapter Eleven

The Trouble With You, Dave, Is You Think Too Big

I am convinced that most high achievers are normal human beings, who discipline themselves to learn and use a variety of skills that result in superior levels of performance.

—Frank Sullivan

It was January 1969, and I was a young, inexperienced manager who had just been asked to take over a small life insurance agency in San Bernardino, California. There were six full-time and four part-time agents working there. Our somewhat unattractive, nine-hundred-square-foot office with linoleum on the floor matched the desks and chairs that had been purchased in the 1950s. It was anything but impressive. On my secretary's desk was a black, manual Royal typewriter, because we couldn't afford a Selectric IBM model, like all the other agencies in town.

I was unsure about a lot of things, but there was one thing I knew: if we wanted to attract high caliber, sharp young agents, we were going to have to do something about our less-than-professional-looking office. Get a picture of this: The outside of our cinder block, single-story building was painted salmon color with turquoise doors. The plants in the planters were always somewhere in the middle of half dead or dying. The parking lot hadn't been resurfaced in years, and the original coat of paint designating the parking stalls was pretty much gone.

We tried a couple of things to dress up our little office. We installed new carpet in the reception area and manager's office, and we updated the reception area furniture. It was a huge improvement compared to what we had started with, but it still was not what we wanted if we were to showcase our goal of becoming the best life insurance agency in town. In order to do that, we had to move from our office's original unimpressive, outdated location to the heart of the downtown financial district.

That idea was easy to plan for, but hard to sell to the home office, who really liked the idea of paying fifty cents a square foot for nine hundred feet of office space. Besides, we were pretty inexperienced, and who could tell whether our new group of young agents would really stick with it? After all, we were asking the company to approve a move into two thousand square feet of office space on the second floor of the Bank of California building, and spend about $25,000 for new furnishings.

I appointed the only other agent in the office, besides me, who looked like he was trying to make a career of it, to be my assistant manager. We decided that we would accomplish two major things in our first year. One, we would both qualify for membership in the prestigious Million Dollar Round Table, and two, we would hire fourteen new agents that year. By the end of that first year, we had done both, and because we knew how to sell, and could go with our new people to show them how to do it the right way, our agency received the President's New Manpower Development Award for paying the most commissions to new agents in their first year.

We were amazed. Our stuff worked. We were doing good. We were being recognized by the home office for having exceptional results. But we still had to sell them on approving our agency's move to that downtown location.

They had a dilemma on their hands. They were impressed with our results and liked our enthusiastic, hands-on approach to bringing our new people along, but they had reservations about getting into a three-year lease for office space that they thought might not fill up in a hurry. Meanwhile, we were all stuffed into that little cracker-box office and were literally bursting at the seams with our fourteen new "winner" recruits. Space was becoming an issue. So the head office people decided to come down and take a first-hand look at where we were and where we wanted to be.

That morning, I was very nervous when the Superintendent of Agencies, the Marketing Vice President, and the President of the company himself, all arrived. As I walked everybody through the new facility, I explained our growth plans and our vision to be the best agency in the whole area. They asked lots of questions, gave us a little static, and wondered why we couldn't still move downtown, but into a smaller space in another location.

I asked them if they liked our results for the first year. They did. I asked if they wanted to have a profitable, professional agency that would be the flagship agency in the company. After a little eye-rolling because of our inexperience, they agreed that they also wanted that, but they had some reservations about that happening very soon. I then responded with that classic line: "If you continue to do what you've always done, you'll continue to get what you've always got."

They were pretty much silent as we left the office and made our way to the parking lot, as the President needed to get to his next meeting. As we walked to his car, the President continued asking questions about whether I thought our growth plans were realistic. As he opened the car door, he turned to me and said: "The trouble with you, Dave, is you think too big. Go ahead and have the bank send a lease agreement to our legal department, and if they're satisfied with it, we'll approve your move."

My assistant manager and I stood there in the parking lot looking casual on the outside as we waved good-bye, but screaming at one hundred and eighty decibels on the inside. We knew that we had just taken a big step to becoming that company's number one agency.

Early in my management career, I wasn't remotely interested in being part of that big group of managers that seemed content with their average, no-growth results. They seemed like the perfect example of those described by Henry David Thoreau when he said: "The mass of men lead lives of quiet desperation."

We were determined to be the best agency in the city and the best agency in the company. It was true that we were young and inexperienced, and I would step on a few landmines over the next couple of years as I learned what was necessary to make our dream a reality, but we were not shy about getting on with it.

There is a concise piece of wisdom I learned in those early days that bears repeating: "Before I became a pro, I acted like one, and by acting like one, I became one." That line resonated with me and my ability to get things done. It motivated me and my management team to do things differently than most of our management peers, both within the company and throughout the industry.

I like Jack Welch's perspective on doing it differently than everyone else. In his book *Winning*, this former head of GE, said: "If there is one … value that really pushes buttons, it is differentiation. Some people love the idea; they swear by it, run their companies with it, and will tell you it is at the very root of their success.

When it is all said and done, differentiation is just resource allocation, which is what good leaders do and, in fact, is one of the chief jobs they are paid to do. A company has only so much money and managerial time. Winning leaders invest where the payback is the highest. They cut their losses everywhere else.

I am convinced that along with being the most efficient and most effective way to run your company, differentiation also happens to be the fairest and the kindest. Ultimately, it makes winners out of everyone."[15]

So, you're asking yourself, what do the early days of managing a small life insurance agency have to do with Jack Welch's approach to managing the giant GE, and this whole business of differentiation? Only this: whether your organization is new or old, large or small, the fact is there are some pure principles of organizational growth and development that never change. For example, those principles include the differentiation between getting "the wrong people off your bus" and getting "the right people on your bus."

That seems simple enough. After all, who wants "wrong

people" fussing and cluttering up their organization in the first place? But it has been amazing to observe that far too many managers hold on to marginal people, instead of terminating their contracts. This usually happens when there is no working plan to regularly recruit new people. Consequently, the manager seeks to exaggerate the activities and results of the organization in order to please his boss, even though such activity is usually pretty transparent.

In the mind of such managers, the attempt is part of a contest which justifies the rationale of keeping the marginal producer around. When the organization embraces poor performance and creates a space for those who are uncommitted to top quality, the manager has betrayed the mission statement of the group, and loses credibility with those in the agency who are, in fact, committed and totally productive. When that happens, productive, determined, and successful people start looking for a better environment to expand their careers, and our mystified manager ends up wondering what could have been done differently to hold on to good people. The manager's "bunker mentality" stands in the way of seeing the problem clearly, and by virtue of being bogged down in the "thick of thin things," this manager ends up living a life of quiet desperation, while his immediate superiors are saying: "The trouble with you is that you don't think very big."

Thinking big does not take a special gift. Its only requirements are desire, commitment, and dedication to the vision you have: that you are going to do things that average men and women cannot do.

Our very best people literally said, "I am only one individual; I can't do everything, but still I can do what I set my mind to do. And even though I can't do everything, I will discipline myself to do those things that are realistic and practical for me, based on my education and experience."

We found that when men and women think like that, they are able see things as they *really* are, instead of how they wished they were. From that perspective, they changed the way they thought about their career and obtained the purpose, commitment, and a dedication to doing whatever it took to accomplish the objective for which they had begun their quest. These people believe in the principle of attraction, and gather around themselves only those positive individuals who have the same kind of focus and commitment that they have. They know that organization and time control are vital to their success, and they spend 90 percent of their time in "quadrant one" thinking, concentrating on the urgent and important. They allocate their time in such a way as to take care of important things and delegate everything else that doesn't require immediate attention.

Back in 1981, after a humiliating early exit from the NBA playoffs, the Los Angeles Lakers found themselves in the midst of a relatively destructive blue funk. Negative attitudes surfaced, accompanied by finger-pointing, fault-finding, jealousy, and back-stabbing. Their new coach, Paul Westhead, was coming under fire in the L.A. press and regularly found himself in some kind of conflict with his best players. By mid-November, during a meeting between Westhead and Magic Johnson, the latter expressed his desire to be traded. His comments sparked a bombshell.

The following morning, the Lakers announced that they were firing one of the best "technical" coaches in the league, not because he wasn't a good coach, but because of his inability to communicate, inspire, and lead. When Pat Riley took over as head coach, he probably wasn't a better coach than Paul Westhead, but he had what Westhead lacked, the great gift of leadership. Pat Riley knew how to listen, assess, guide, and motivate. He knew that if he could get the best from each and every player, they could play like a beautiful orchestra, with each player not only knowing his part but doing it in such a way that it was harmonious with every other player, who also knew and did his part. It would be athletic beauty at its best.

These were lofty ideals that would take time to prove, but Riley had inherited a team that was in chaos. Coaching basketball and managing a group of high energy, large ego sales types, have the same kind of chaotic challenges. Riley soon learned that it was vital for him to understand exactly what motivated his best players, before he could determine how he and they were going to solve their big mutual problem.

With that perspective, he went to Kareem first and told him that the only way the Lakers could hold together as a team was if he would take responsibility to be their leader. Kareem's perfect response was "I can play for you, don't worry about me." It was as simple as that, and was all that Riley needed. Kareem was there. He was with him.

But it was a little more complex dealing with the other members of the team. Magic Johnson, Nixon, and Cooper were loaded with talent and had some pretty strong egos which required a lot of massaging and recognition. While it was true that they were pretty close friends, their individual needs were overriding that friendship, and creating a little controversy, between them.

Riley began to sell them on the idea that they could become the best guard combination in the history of the NBA. He told them that instead of fighting each other, "they should want to be godfathers to each others' children ... that's how close you ought to be." They bought it, and for a while, it worked perfectly. That small picture of how it could be, made all the difference.

They responded by winning twelve of the next fourteen games they played. All their statistics improved dramatically, and like Riley hoped, they began to play together in complete harmony.

The press began to call it "show time," everybody wanted to see it, and see it they did! It was an incredible year which culminated in another NBA Championship.

Only six months earlier, that same team had begun the season in total chaos, losing six out of eight games; there had been no chemistry and everybody on the team had been burdened with a "me first" mentality. How could a team make this kind of turnaround? They did it because they inherited a leader, instead of a manager, in the person of Pat Riley, who based his personal foundation on always "thinking big."

As you've noticed, the lack of organizational commitment is what keeps employees in many of this country's businesses, from living up to their potential and it's one of the big reasons why so many organizations have become "run of the mill" and uninspiring. Now more than ever before, it's clear that organizational commitment and teamwork is the key to real competitiveness. The problem is that people have become cynical as a result of all the downsizing, and new rules, that have changed once "great places to work," into "just a job." The employees in such companies, are unwilling or afraid to act with commitment, because they don't know if the company will commit to them in a reciprocal way.

In the end, no matter who the major stock holders are, and no matter who the managers are, in essence, the company belongs to those employees who make and keep commitment, and who get the big job done. The leader's job is literally to serve those who demonstrate such loyalty. When that happens, an environment is created where talent can flourish. That's the job of those who claim to be great in the business of leading others. They are able to so because they are somehow able to think big and inspire others to do the same.

The building of your company is really very simple. Treat your people the way you would want to be treated if the roles were reversed and they will move heaven and earth for you. Riley's ability to build one of the greatest dynasties in the history of professional basketball and your desire to build one of the best companies in your industry are based on the same thing: Your ability to think big, be courageous, forget your own ego and be a light to your people. The results will be beyond your wildest dreams.

Here's the lesson:

- Don't be afraid to think big.
- Don't be satisfied with being average—be exceptional.
- Act like a pro.
- Winning leaders invest where the payoff is the highest.
- A leader creates an environment where talent can flourish.

Chapter Twelve

You Are Never Going to Be the Same

The reason opportunity is not often recognized is because it is very often disguised as hard work.

—G. Carey Hauenstein

Isn't it fascinating that no one remains the same? Nobody stands still. Like our muscles, we either get stronger or we atrophy. No one remains just as they are. Has your tennis game deteriorated? How can that be, when you used to be so good at it? Remember when you were a high school athlete? You got to the place where you were so good at your sport that on game day, there was no thinking about how to dribble the ball, shoot the ball, pass the ball, or hit the ball. Everything was complete reaction, based on hours, days, weeks, months, and years of practice. If your sport wasn't basketball, tennis, baseball, or track, it doesn't matter. Was it not true that by the time you got really good at it, you never had to think about what you were going to do next because everything had become automatic reaction?

Maybe you didn't excel in sports; maybe your interest was in music, or fixing cars, or learning everything under the sun about computers. It doesn't matter. The principles are still the same. Over time, you finally got to the place where you didn't have to think about the next step to take; it had become simple reaction to the events.

And so here we are now early in the twenty-first century. Are you better at the business of running your business, or are you starting to slip a little? If it's the latter, it's time to determine if you are treating your business with the same respect and dedication that you treat your golf game, your tennis game, or whatever else you are passionate about. If you are going to survive and grow over the next decade, you need to take a deep breath and decide right now if you are willing to "retool" to improve the way your business gets done. In short, are you willing to step up and lead?

Warren Bennis, the distinguished professor of Business Administration and the Chairman of the Leadership Institute at the University of Southern California, said: "To survive in the 21st century, we'll need a new generation of leaders, not managers. The distinction is an important one. Leaders conquer the context—the volatile, turbulent, ambiguous surroundings that sometimes seem to conspire against us and will surely suffocate us if we let them—while managers surrender to it. There are other differences as well, and they are crucial:

- The manager administers; the leader innovates.
- The manager is a copy; the leader is an original.
- The manager maintains; the leader develops.
- The manager relies on control; the leader inspires trust.

- The manager has a short-range view; the leader has a long-range perspective.

- The manager asks how and when; the leader asks what and why.

- The manager has his or her eye on the bottom line; the leader has his eye on the horizon.

- The manager accepts the status quo; the leader challenges it.

- The manager is the classic good soldier; the leader is his or her own person.

- The manager does things right; the leader does the right thing.

I've spent twenty years talking with leaders, close to 1,000 men and women, some famous and some not. In the process, I've learned something about the current crop of leaders and something about the leadership that will be necessary to forge the future. While leaders come in every size, shape and disposition—short, tall, neat, sloppy, young, old, male and female—every leader I talked with shared at least one characteristic: a concern with the guiding purpose, an overarching vision. They were more than goal-directed. Leaders have a clear idea of what they want to do and the strength to persist in the face of setbacks, even failures. They know where they are going and why."8

How Does Your Organization Compare?

Look around. How do you stack up against Bennis's list? Are you and your organization up to date?

- Are you in touch with what the best in your industry are doing?

- Do you know how they got to be the best?

- When you compare everything about the way they do business, how they recruit and train and what kind of retention rate they have, how do you stack up?

- Do you attend your industry's best educational functions and seminars, and are your top management people with you?

- Do you subscribe to the industry's best magazines, periodicals, and newsletters, and do you actually read them to keep current on what the latest is for other companies in your business?

- How does your marketing strategy compare to the marketing strategies of the top companies and organizations in your industry?

The great companies in your industry do this, and as a consequence, they thrive, grow, and become more profitable every year. The growth and productivity of your organization will only improve if you learn the answers to these questions. It may be that there are some major changes to complete—serious surgery may be required. Or it may be that only some technique refinement is what's needed to get where you want to be. The more serious matter to consider is whether you and your management team have the vision, the drive, and the discipline necessary to carefully plan the strategy and then follow the roadmap required to take your company in a different direction. If there are members of your team who drag their feet at the prospect of change, bid them good-bye.

Work with only positive, goal-oriented people who share your vision and have the guts to do whatever it takes to succeed.

All leaders guide their followers' vision and provide clearly-marked road maps. The result then is that every member can see in which direction the corporation is going. The communication of the vision generates excitement about the trip. The plans for the journey create order out of chaos, instill confidence and trust, and offer criteria for success. The group knows when it has arrived.

If you're not sure of your company's vision, how can you tell what the advantages of an alliance would be? You must be certain you have the right map before embarking on the journey.

Consider these questions from Bennis: "If you think your company's vision lacks definition, here are some questions that may help give it color and dimension:

- What is unique about us?
- What values are true priorities this year?
- What would make me professionally commit my mind and heart to this vision over the next five to ten years?
- What does the world really need that our company can and should provide?
- What do I want our company to accomplish so that I will be committed, aligned, and proud of my association with the institution?

Ask yourself those questions. Your answers will be the fire that heats the forge of your company's future."[8]

We went through several such question-and-answer

sessions when we were trying to decide exactly what had to be done to move our organization from just average to one of the best in the industry. The changes that were required of us were sometimes painful, but the result was well worth it.

We knew what we wanted to become, but we weren't sure how to get there, so we spent a lot of time asking others, who had been more successful than we were, what they did to get where they were. We found that careful listening to their answers was essential.

Not all outwardly successful companies are filled with integrity. Not all outwardly successful companies have a corporate culture that you'll feel good about emulating. As you know, there are a lot of seemingly successful organizations out there that are basically in the "shooting star" phase of business, but their long-term, sustainable growth is yet to be proven.

So, be wise in your quest to learn what the "best" companies are doing; be sure that they really are among the best. If you have no way of knowing that, just be sure that you don't fall in love with a "pretty face." If I were you, I'd be asking direct questions like:

- Tell me about your company's mission statement.
- Tell me about *your* mission statement.
- Tell me about your recruiting procedures and the kind of new recruit you're looking for.

Questions such as these, and more, will reveal the organizational culture, and allow you to accurately assess if there is anything in this company that is worth adopting.

Be patient with the process. Stay focused and make

commitments that you try to accomplish, so that when you become weary, your integrity will hold you to the task at hand. In the process of changing some of what you do, in an effort to accomplish greater things, don't lose your own personality or individuality.

When I adopted Tommie Smith's workout in my college days, I didn't actually do "everything" he was doing. For one thing, I was a better starter than he was, and so I did not change my starting technique, nor did I change the way I took and gave baton handoffs in the 400-meter relay. Our results in the NCAA 400-meter relay race earned us All-American status. So don't forget who you are in your quest to improve. Hold on to your "best self," and change only the things that are keeping you from accomplishing what you truly want.

This little vignette from Pulitzer Prize winner Jules Feiffer sums it up pretty well:

"Ever since I was a little kid, I didn't want to be me. I wanted to be Billie Widdledon, and Billy Widdledon didn't even like me. I walked like "he" walked, I talked like "he" talked, I signed up for the high school "he" signed up for.

Which is when Widdleton changed. He began to hang around Herby Vandeman. He walked like Herby Vandeman; he talked like Herby Vandeman; he mixed me up. I began to walk and talk like Billie Widdledon walking and talking like Herby Vandeman.

Then it dawned on me that Herby Vandeman walked and talked like Joey Haverlin, and Joey Haverlin walked and talked like Corky Sabinson. So here I am walking and talking like Billie Widdledon's imitation of Herby Vandeman's version of Joey Haverlin trying to walk and talk like Corky Sabinson.

And WHO do you think Corky Sabinson is always walking and talking like? Of *all* people, Dopey Wellington—that little pest, who walks and talks like ... me."[17]

Here's the lesson:

- The manager maintains; the leader develops.
- Leaders have a clear idea of what they want to do and the strength to persist in the face of setbacks, or even failures.
- You must know what the best in your industry do that makes them the best.
- The single defining quality of leaders is their capacity to create and realize a vision.
- Make sure you have the right map before embarking on the journey.

Chapter Thirteen

To Thine Own Self Be True

If I care more about an agent's problems than he does, then he's in the wrong business, or at least in the wrong agency.

—David Reeves

In my junior year in high school, our English teacher introduced us to Shakespeare. To my surprise, I really enjoyed it. One of Shakespeare's most-often quoted lines comes from Hamlet. As his son Laertis is about to depart, Polonius gives him some of the best fatherly advice any son ever received: "This above all: To thine own self be true, and it must follow, as the night the day, thou canst not then be false to any man."

I grew up in a household where my parents taught their eight children the value of honesty and integrity. The fruits of that teaching were exemplified in the life of my father. I often heard other men speak of the great respect they had for him because they could always depend on his word. If he said it was so—it was so. He never exaggerated or failed to disclose. He never misled anyone.

Consequently, early in my business career, it was very easy for me to make this phrase into the central theme of my own personal mission statement: "I would treat my client the way I'd want to be treated if the roles were reversed." I came to gain so much respect for the truly great ones in my industry, who had also crafted their mission statement upon similar concepts, if not nearly identical words. As they did that, they were formulating the way to stay true to themselves.

One of the Great Ones:

As a young college student in the sixties, one of the greatest collegiate basketball players I ever saw played for Utah State University. His name was Wayne Estes and he stood six foot six. In his senior year he was the second leading scorer in the nation, right behind the great Rick Barry, averaging 33.7 points a game, and 13.7 rebounds. There was no better basketball player west of the Mississippi, and none more popular.

Wayne Estes was from Anaconda, Montana, and he was everybody's hero. After basketball games, whether at home or on the road, he would often spend as much as thirty minutes signing autographs, talking to kids, and encouraging them about their game.

What most people do not know about Wayne Estes is the personal integrity he had as he disciplined himself to do things that others wouldn't do. Every day after practice, when the others had gone to shower and dress, he would stay on the basketball court and shoot, sometimes for an hour or more, from the ten favorite spots on the floor that he had marked with tape. He would shoot until he made it ten times from that spot, and then move to the next. It wasn't always easy, and it was usually painful because of fatigue. But integrity was the driving force that made him do it every day, and the result was his prolific scoring ability and the recognition that pronounced him the best pure shooter ever.

During the Christmas season of 1964, Utah State played a holiday tournament in Hawaii. Wayne scored fifty-two points against Boston College, was named tournament MVP, and was congratulated by their coach as being the best basketball player he had ever seen. Bob Cousy was there; after the game, he told him, "You have great hands; I think you can make it in the NBA." But Wayne never played one minute in the NBA.

On February 8, 1965, Utah State was playing at home against the University of Denver. In that game Estes scored forty-eight points, shooting twenty of twenty-eight from the field, and breaking the Utah State University single season scoring record with his 2001st point.

He spent twenty minutes afterward signing autographs and kids' basketballs. From there, he went back to his dorm, and then off he went for some pizza, with a couple of buddies. On their way back, they saw a car accident near campus. As they approached the accident scene, Wayne did not see that the accident had bent a power pole that caused the power line to drop to about six feet, four inches off the ground. Wayne never saw the line, and being six foot six, he walked right into it and was electrocuted.

The Utah State University family was stunned and grief-stricken beyond words, as was the entire town of Anaconda and the state of Montana. Four days later, Wayne's funeral service was held in his old, high school gym. Words of both sorrow and praise were spoken. The minister's concluding remarks were both poetic and *á propos*, in honor of this great and beloved athlete: "So live your life that in the hour of your death, all others will be weeping and you will be the only one without a tear to shed. Then you shall calmly face death whenever and wherever it comes."[18]

While it's true that Wayne Estes was a great basketball player, he was an even better person. I am confident that he had no tear to shed as he moved on to greater things, because the integrity of his life had taken him to the greatest accomplishments that any athlete could hope for. But this story is not about basketball. This story is that he was true to himself, his principles, his integrity, and his ability to make a difference in the lives of others.

Honest, Simple, Solid, True

I know a man by the name of C. Terry Warner, a distinguished professor of philosophy. In a 1996 gathering of university students, he gave a talk titled, "Honest, Simple, Solid, True." In that talk he shared some soul-searching insight into his younger life. I found some of myself in his anecdotes. Perhaps you will too.

Terry stuttered badly most of the way through school. When he tried to answer questions in class, he was seldom successful. We've all seen the grimace a stutterer makes with flickering eyelids, accompanied by the strained expressions on people's faces.

As children often do, he compensated by became brash, loud, boastful, and competitive. This put people off, a response which only made him try harder to win their acceptance.

As the years went by, he made good progress overcoming the stuttering, and people treated him better. But he was still troubled. He was often pitted against others; he was driven to get a bigger share and felt distrustful and scornful of certain people.

He said that he caught himself trying to arrange himself in the minds of others, playing a role, posturing. Every year he spoke more smoothly, but still he couldn't close the gap between the fabricated image he presented publicly and who he really was.

Warner was going to school in Manhattan and taking classes in theater. By then, he was in his early twenties, and in spite of being in the midst of millions of people, he often felt alone because of the façade behind which he was hiding.

One evening a classmate confronted him with a terrifying question. "Do you love yourself in the theater, or the theater in yourself?" She was asking whether he was in theater to promote himself, or simply because he loved it.

The question convicted him—perhaps because the theater makes a tempting platform for posturing. He recalled wishing that all his pretensions would collapse completely, and leave only the real Terry Warner standing. It did not matter any longer whether he would impress anyone or not—*If only … if only he could be honest, simple, solid, and true.*

Warner began a personal quest in that direction, but whatever changes took place in him didn't last long, and the same challenge kept returning in new forms. A couple of years later, he had some experiences that began to strip some of the veneer away. But in spite of that, he really wasn't making much progress at all.

The problem didn't lie in his objectives; those were pretty lofty and consisted of being scrupulously honest, never compromising principles, and always standing up for what he felt was right. But he was pursuing his objectives for himself.

Although he couldn't see it then, in a very subtle way his quest continued the very self-preoccupation that he was trying to overcome, which twisted the goal of being true into being true *to himself*, and for his own sake.

No matter how rigorous a quest to be true is, when someone undertakes it on their own behalf, it can never put to silence the disquieting voice that says, "You're not honest, simple, solid, and true. You're still in it for yourself. It's your own agenda that you care about most."

In his life-long quest to become completely honest and simple, Warner finally realized that in order to respond to the needs of others, it was essential that he forget himself.

Did you see any part of yourself in Terry Warner's story? I did, and like him, the success I sought did not fully come until I felt the need to make a difference in the lives of others.

The real leaders I have known have the capacity to not only be true to themselves, but to care passionately about the needs of others. Whatever their responsibilities true leaders seek to make a difference.

When my associates and I decided to rise above the ordinary level of performance that was so prevalent in our industry, we learned that being true to ourselves and our lofty aspirations meant being true to others and putting them first. We found that when we did, our needs took care of themselves.

He Could Use Me Any Day

There is a wonderful story about an old English sea captain who was dying. At his bedside was his old friend, a New York newspaper editor. They reminisced about old times, and then the editor asked his friend: "What changed your life? We were pretty wild in our youth. Something changed us. What changed you? Was it that experience you had out there in the ocean when the *Casper* was sinking and you rescued all who were aboard?"

The old captain said: "Yes, that's where it happened. Seemed impossible to get anybody off the *Casper* before she broke in two and went down. But we got them all off. Half dozen times we almost went down ourselves. But we got them all off."

The captain of the *Casper* was the last one, and I was holding his four-year-old daughter when he climbed up the deck ladder and come over the rail to my boat. His wife was weeping, and she said to her husband, "See, I told you that God had talked to me and told me that everybody was going to be saved."

She then held out her hands to take her daughter from my arms. The little girl snuggled up closer to me, and I had a three-to-four-days growth of beard, but she put her cheek against mine and said, "Mother, is this God?"

The mother smiled and said, "No honey, what makes you think he is God?"

"Well, you kept saying that God would save us. This man saved us."

The mother said, "No honey, he is not God. He is just one of God's men that He used today."

The old sea captain turned to his boyhood friend with a radiant light and heaven in his eyes. "You know," he said, "I just decided I'd be one of God's men always. He could use me any day. He could use me every day if he wanted to. It changed my life."

Applause Naturally Comes

We learned that being true to ourselves, while being concerned with the needs of others is the ultimate achievement that requires total integrity. Such personal integrity is found in the very nature of authentic leaders and is the first step to true greatness. To maintain it in high places costs self denial, but its end is glorious.

The difficulty comes when our accomplishments become part of our personality, and we start "strutting our stuff." We start reading our "press clippings" and believing them. We start saying, "Mirror, mirror on the wall, who's the fairest of them all?" And we believe that the mirror is going to answer back, "You are!" That's about the time the wheels fall off.

We found that there's no need to seek the applause. The applause comes naturally to great achievement. The trick is to maintain humility and not forget where you came from. There's nothing worse than the egocentric individual who needs to hear applause and regularly fishes for it.

When you accomplish great things, be glad. Share it with your spouse and even your best friend. If you are asked to speak about it, do that with the kind of humility that former Michigan Governor George Romney did, when he was asked to speak to a national meeting where he was receiving their "Man of the Year" Award. He was asked to tell how he had turned American Motors around. As he began to speak, he said, "It's always difficult to talk about yourself without creating impressions you don't want to create." He then went on to tell what happened. And even though we all knew that none of that turnaround would have happened without him, he gave all the credit for the success to everyone else that had been involved. George Romney knew who he was and what he had accomplished. That was good enough for him.

The opening lines of Edgar A. Guest's poem, *Myself*, focus on being true to yourself:

> I have to live with myself and so
> I want to be fit for myself to know.
> I want to be able as days go by,
> to look at myself straight in the eye.

This classic poem convicts those who impudently disregard the virtues of honesty, loyalty, and fair play. It's true that there are countless individuals whose moral compass is so far off true north that they rationalize that impudence; they will probably never find their way back. Be wise. Real leaders do not work or think with that perspective. Don't get sucked into going with the flow. Be true to your best self. Be a light to those around you who need the example of a leader such as you. Consider the concluding lines of *Myself*:

> I know what others may never know,
> I cannot fool myself and so,
> Whatever happens, I want to be
> Self-respecting and conscience free.

Here's the lesson:

- I treat my client the way I'd want to be treated if the roles were reversed.
- Live your life so that when you die, others will be weeping and you will be the only one without a tear to shed.
- Integrity is one of several paths, but it distinguishes itself from the others because it is the right path, and the only one upon which you will never get lost.
- A leader is honest, simple, solid, and true.

Chapter Fourteen

If I Don't Do it, Who Will?

Recognize that in your business you only have one reputation.
It is either a good one, and it helps you, or it's not so good and it
hurts you. Your integrity and reputation are everything.

—Monroe Diefendorf

Two thousand years ago the Jewish Rabbi Hillel said: "If I don't do it, who will? If I don't do it now, when will I? If I do it only for myself, who am I?"[19]

These are profound questions that are part of the foundation one must build in order to rise above the ego needs that are common to most men. The answers to those questions are found in the lives and character of those who assume the responsibilities of leadership.

The key word in these three questions is the word "I." It is the key word here because it focuses on the personal responsibility that all those who claim the role of leader must be willing to take. In reference to that kind of responsibility, I like what Jon Huntsman said:

"In the world of business today there are many leaders— certainly in title. However, leadership in the true sense of the word is not so abundant. The top executives of some of the leading businesses haven't the slightest idea of the breadth of stakeholder expectations. That's the result of leaders simply being appointed to the position or who found themselves at the top of a corporate chart, next in line for the top job. Real leadership demands character. Effective, respected leadership is maintained through mutual agreement. Leadership demanded is leadership denied. Leadership is not meant to be dominion over others. Rather, it is the composite of characteristics that earn respect, results, and a continued following."[3]

The reason great leadership is at such a premium is that most people are unwilling to shoulder the full responsibility for the countless programs, people, plans, and goals that every successful company is involved in. Most people are not capable of putting others first because for them, "it's all about *me!*"

In his book *"A New Paradigm of Leadership,"* Ken Shelton cites three leadership perspectives. The first comes from General Robert R. Fogleman, former Joint Chief of Staff for the United States Air force:

"I can say from my military experience that the difference between a good unit and a bad unit is leadership. Where you find poor units, you find poor commanders. In the military, and I suspect also in the corporate world, leadership is the key, because the personnel system, in the aggregate, deals everyone an even hand. Every unit will get some super stars, some middle ground folks, and some who are not up to standards."[8]

The second example that Shelton gives is Peter Drucker, who said that there is no substitute for leadership. He defines leadership simply as "getting things accomplished by acting through others."

Shelton's third reference is Tom Peters. "All excellent companies have strong leaders at every level. When you are put into a leadership position, you need to take stock of your people and get to know them not just as names, but as people. You must treat them with the dignity with which you would like to be treated. That won't always be easy, because you will have people who don't live up to your expectations. But successful leaders know how to make the best use of each talent assigned to them."[8]

After I had been in the business of agency building in Southern California for about seven years, the company asked me to relocate to Provo, Utah, where they had two separate agencies that weren't doing very well. They were combining those two offices into one and wanted me to manage it.

During the first thirty days, I interviewed the twenty-five agents who made up those two agencies that had been assigned to me. I interviewed each of them twice. In those meetings, we discussed where they were in their careers, where they thought they were heading, and what their families thought of insurance and financial services as a career. We talked about where their market was and what they needed the agency to do to help them develop it. I asked them about their commitment to the business and what their goals were. I asked them if they were willing to do every single thing I told them to do, if I promised them that in so doing, they would double their income in the next six months.

Their responses were varied and interesting but mostly disappointing. What I learned about the group was that most of them viewed their relationship with the company as just a job. Only a few believed that it was a career. In response to my questions about their willingness to do everything I told them to do in order to double their income, most expressed cynicism and indicated that they really didn't like being told what to do. I explained that the only things I would tell them to do would directly relate to money-making activities.

At the end of the thirty days, I fired twenty of them and kept five.

Weren't any of them worth keeping? Based on my determination to only gather around me the best I could find, the answer is no. It was essential to set a standard and make that standard clear. The positive effect that decision had on the five that were left was meaningful. We saw an immediate, positive response from the five. Their energy level increased, and so did their production. Most of them became some of our company's best producers. We learned that a focused plan and a committed attitude created a culture within our new little group that was contagious. As those five began to introduce us to others, our growth rate became extraordinary, and within one year we were among the top agencies in the country.

I believe that we have an obligation to the entire organization to keep only those individuals who actually buy into the philosophy and mission statement. If they do not, we need to help them find a new job opportunity. Doing so strengthens our position and improves the morale of the group. In the words of Jim Collins, we got the wrong people off the bus and the right people on the bus. Doing otherwise invites negative attitudes and bad habits to permeate the whole environment.

When terminating an employee's work relationship, there

is no necessity for meanness or lack of compassion—quite to the contrary. It costs nothing to be kind, and the great leaders know that we always reap what we sow.

We found that the real leadership thinks this way:

- When you find a problem, deal with it in a kind, mature, and forthright way.
- Don't use a stick of dynamite when a scalpel will do.
- When there's a problem that needs to be addressed and only one person was responsible for creating it, meet privately with that individual and fix the problem. Getting the whole group together and chewing everyone out, or painting the whole organization with the same brush irritates the group and allows the offending one to share the guilt with everyone else. This is completely counter-productive.

As we discussed problems privately with the actual offender, we learned that we got better results if we were fair, firm, and consistent, and showed that we understood the difference between a major error and a mistake. An honest mistake does not require the same kind of correction that a major error does. Again, don't use a stick of dynamite when a scalpel will do.

Organization and Time Control

In an earlier chapter, I talked about organization and time control. When we reorganized the agency and started over, one of the most important things I taught my young associates was the great necessity of focused, meaningful planning, personal organization, and time control. Those young agents didn't know everything they needed to know to be successful in our business, but they quickly learned the benefits of controlling their time and making short- and long-term decisions. Instilling personal organization at the start of their careers put them miles ahead of their peers as they progressed in their careers.

Perhaps you've heard of American Express's former CFO, Gary Crittenden, and the way he approaches things. Here's what Jeff Benedict had to say about him.

"Crittenden's duties at the world-leading financial services firm are vast. They include: (1) providing leadership to the company's finance group; (2) serving as key adviser on strategic and financial matters world-wide; and (3) representing American Express to investors, lenders, and rating agencies. His typical work day starts 6:15 a.m. and ends when he arrives back home around 8:00 p.m. This amounts to fourteen hours per day, door-to-door, or seventy hours per week; Crittenden spends an additional five hours each Saturday working from his home office.

[Additionally] he's involved in volunteer work for his church, which occupies an additional 15 hours per week.

But the titles Crittenden takes most seriously are those of husband and father. Those obligations have another set of time [commitments] each week.

The ability to maximize work performance while balancing family obligations is the challenge of every working professional. 'Work is all about what you actually deliver and very little about just spending time,' said Crittenden. 'Just putting in time doesn't help you much. It's about figuring out what needs to be done and mobilizing a larger organization to make it happen. If you can do that, you have a lot of flexibility in how you use your time. The better you do that over time, the more time and flexibility you have.'

To fulfill his obligations to his family, his company, and his church, Crittenden follows some basic rules:

- Do the most important things first.
- Do the urgent things second.
- Delegate the things that are not urgent.
- Skip altogether the things that are unimportant.

The trick, Crittenden said, is distinguishing between what's most important and what's urgent. It will never be urgent to put Easter eggs in the yard with my grandson, but it can be very important. So the question is what are the truly important things that I want to achieve in life, and how do I plan those into my calendar first to ensure those things get done? Then you have to deal with the urgent things that are important, typically because they arise at work."[20]

It always surprises me when I hear people say that organization and time control are just for those who are slaves to their calendar. We learned it was just the opposite. By being fully calendared, I was freed from the anxiety of wondering if I was missing something. Consequently, I was never late to, or missed meetings. I was always available to help my people, and I was still able to be at the kids' plays, little league games, and all other kinds of family time, without sacrificing the important or the urgent parts of my business.

Those who "wing it," and work from memory only or from little pieces of paper are out of date; they are under self-imposed pressure that could be completely eliminated if they were wise enough to do it the Crittenden way. To operate your life in any other manner promises frustration at work for you and your people, and at home for you and your family.

By doing business and conducting our personal family time in this manner, our accomplishments were significant, and as a management team, we were exemplary to our agents while still being able to provide them with the assistance promised.

Albert E. N. Gray said it best: "Successful men form the habit of doing things that failures will not do." If this affirmation is difficult for you to embrace, just think back to what you know about your own personal successes in whatever forum you were in. Isn't it true that you proved Gray's declaration yourself, but possibly never verbalized it in this precise way?

An unknown author said this: "The quality of a person's work is never an accident. It is the result of high intentions, sincere effort, intelligent direction, and knowledgeable execution. It represents the wise choice of many alternatives. Every job is a self-portrait of the individual who did it." I have always tried to autograph my work with excellence.

As it turned out, Hillel's questions were a valuable part of our philosophy and mission statement, and although I'm no Gary Crittenden, I have always tried to apply these words to the way I work with both my business associates and our clients. "If I don't do it, who will?" was part of the way we autographed our work and related to our people. Along the way, there were always those who wanted to know how we accomplished the things we did. It wasn't just hard work. We created a loyalty in the relationships we had with every one of our employees, consequently they did better-than-average things that helped us accomplish our goal of being the number one agency in the company.

Here's the lesson:

- Real leadership demands character.
- Work is all about what you actually deliver and very little about just spending time.
- A key to prioritizing time commitments is knowing when to say "no."
- Every job is a self-portrait of the individual who did it.

Chapter Fifteen

You Can Count on Me

When faced with the question, "What should I do?" the answer is, "Do what's right." When faced with the question, "What's right?" the answer is,"Treat the other person the way you'd want to be treated if the roles were reversed."

—Lou Holtz

Early in my career, it became painfully clear that not everyone in my industry was "Honest, simple, solid, and true." I observed that the insurance-buying public generally had that same opinion. I didn't like that. I wanted to be respected for the way I conducted business, and I was being painted by the same brush that was painting those who approached their careers with expediency in my industry. I couldn't solve this industry-wide problem, but I did demonstrate to my clients that, unlike others they had dealt with in the past, I was the "value added."

I demonstrated that at the start of every interview. After some pleasant introductory conversation, the dialogue went something like this: "Before we get underway here today, let me just say one very important thing ... relax. The reason I want you to relax is that I have nothing to sell you. The reason

I have nothing to sell you is because I don't know where you are financially. I don't know where you're heading, and I don't know where you *want to be heading* financially. Those three things are always different. And because I don't know any of that, I couldn't possibly suggest that you buy something, just because you came here today.

"What I'd like to do while we're together, is to ask you about fifty questions to learn where you are and where you want to be … financially. Then I'd like to keep that information for about a week, and tear it down into its little component parts, and put it back together in kind of a priority order. Then I'd like you to come back. I'll have a list of recommendations, based on what you told me, about where you are and where you're heading financially. You'll examine the list. There may be one or two things that won't fit, but the rest will tend to fit you just like a glove.

"When you come back, the worst thing that will happen is that you'll decide to do nothing. If that happens, that's O.K., we'll still like you. And if it's O.K. with you, I'll probably call you a year from now and ask if we can talk about it again. Would it be alright if we proceeded on that basis?"

It was always "alright," because at that point, my potential clients trusted me and knew there wasn't going to be any high-pressure salesmanship to endure. They were willing to tell me everything I needed to know in order to help me make recommendations that would fit their needs.

Of all the things that we taught our associates over the years, there was one thing that we taught and demanded more than anything else. "Treat your client the way you'd want to be treated."

Not only that, but we taught our people to "love what you do, do what you love, and deliver more than you promise." As I said in an earlier chapter, the necessity of it was so important to us that it served to help develop the organizational mission statement and affirmation: "What I do is exceedingly different, I will treat my client the way I'd want to be treated if the roles were reversed." We believed it and acted accordingly.

In the course of developing the personal financial planning strategies that my clients sought, I continued to assure them: "When you do this work with us, you get me in the bargain. Today it may not be clear to you what a valuable asset that is, but as time goes by, you will know it and be grateful for it." As time went by, our clients did know it and were extremely grateful for it. You can imagine the difference that made in the relationships we developed with every client. They knew that they could trust us.

Some might say: "Well, it's a lot easier to conduct business with a client one-on-one, because then the stakes are not as high as when people are making multi-million-dollar business decisions in Fortune 500 companies." But we didn't see it that way. Our position was that it didn't make any difference if the client was prepared to spend three hundred dollars, one million dollars, or one hundred million dollars. The high trust that is developed in every single business relationship operates with this "client first" mentality, and that's the mentality that makes the business thrive, grow, and last. Nordstrom, Ritz-Carlton, JetBlue, Southwest Airlines, Northwestern Mutual, and Costco, to name only a few examples, prove it over and over again.

If you doubt that, just ask yourself the question, "What

caused the financial disasters at Enron, Tyco, WorldCom, Arthur Anderson, and Fannie Mae," just to name those five? Most of what was behind those corporate scandals can be reduced to two words: dishonesty and greed. Not only did those companies "hit the wall" financially, but in the process, thousands of employees lost their jobs as well as their retirement plans. Not only that, but countless thousands of investors, both institutional and individual, lost millions of dollars they will never get back.

Over the past several years, we have seen a continual stream of major companies restating their earnings, allowing fraudulent accounting procedures, and artificially hyping the value of their stock.

Because such practices are not uncommon, it is even more impressive to consider why the former CEO of Dell Computers was so well respected. That respect was earned by demonstrating his personal quest for total integrity. It wasn't something he'd developed over the years; it's what he was. Integrity was like a second skin to him; everyone knew that they could trust Kevin Rollins. A story about a business venture in his college days is a classic:

"While an undergraduate student, Rollins started a soft-drink company called Pop Shoppe. It distributed beverages throughout the state. On one occasion, Rollins had contracted to purchase a larger order of custom-made soft-drink bottles from a supplier. A competing supplier subsequently approached Rollins and offered to supply the bottles for a much lower price.

At that point, the first supplier had already begun making the custom bottles. 'But we could have canceled, and there would have been nothing the first supplier could have done. They would have been stuck with the bottles.'

Legally, Rollins could have backed out of the first contract.

'We could have gotten a better deal and more money, but we had made a commitment to those folks. We would have had to leave them hanging in order to go with the other supplier. And we couldn't do that.'

Rollins notified the second supplier of his decision in a conversation that he recalled went like this:

'Sorry, we've already made the order. We're committed.'

'Well, you can cancel it.'

'No, we can't. We already made the commitment.'"[20]

I wonder, but of course we'll never know, what kind of company Enron could have become if its leaders had been willing to treat their employees, suppliers, and investors with the same selfless integrity that Kevin Rollins demonstrated? Think of the difference it would have made in the lives of hundreds of thousands of people.

One of the most successful individuals in the insurance industry is relatively unknown. His name is Rod Hawes. Along with two partners he founded the world's largest, privately-owned life reinsurance company. He was the CEO of that company until it sold for nearly two billion dollars. His rural, close-family upbringing taught him many valuable lessons, but none was more important than personal integrity. When asked his perspective on high trust in the real world of business, he replied:

"By building relationships of trust with CEOs and executives throughout the industry, Hawes carried out hundreds of millions of dollars in mergers and acquisitions on the basis of a handshake. 'I had no written agreements with these people … integrity is a key part of the deal. I'm not tolerant when it comes to people who lie, people who cheat, and people who don't tell the truth. That's a no-no. If you have a problem, you can tell me anything. I can deal with any problem. But don't lie to me.'"[20]

Not only does Rod Hawes tolerate no nonsense when it comes to the truth, he is also the consummate leader when it comes to his relationships with his employees. Consider how he treats those who work for him and ponder how different corporate America would be today if the top people at Enron, Tyco, and WorldCom had embraced Rod Hawes' way of taking care of their employees. Here's how Jeff Benedict describes Hawes:

As CEO, Hawes believed that his company would perform better if his employees were treated fairly and compensated appropriately. In 1992, when Hawes took his private company public, he insisted that every employee be given stock in the company. "Everyone right down to the clerk in the mailroom got stock," said Hawes. "I don't understand people who are so selfish and greedy that they feel entitled to squeeze other people. I just don't get it. First of all, it's stupid from a business standpoint because you can get much more out of employees when you are good to them."[20]

In the early days of building successful agencies, it was our practice to always treat every employee with respect. Not only was this our practice with our sales force, who was our financial life blood, but it was especially so with our secretaries and executive assistants. No bossing people around. No bullying. Just "treating them the way we wanted to be treated."

Nobody gets paid enough to put up with rude, thoughtless behavior. If it was ever reported to me that an agent had been verbally abusive to a secretary, I would immediately call that person to my office to learn "what and why." Invariably, the agent had reacted to a problem in an immature manner. I would deal with the matter showing the same respect that I wanted the agent to give a secretary, so there were no threats or brow-beating, but merely a directive to go to the secretary, privately apologize for the thoughtless behavior, and assure her that she should expect to never be treated that way again.

I instructed our office staff to never put up with any kind of harassment or abuse from any of our people, or for that matter from any of our clients. I instructed them to put upset or verbally-abusive clients on hold and turn them over to me. I could then smooth ruffled feathers and resolve the client's concerns. When my staff knew that they could enjoy such protection in their job, it helped strengthen their loyalty.

We had an associate who didn't think it mattered how he treated his assistants or our secretaries. In spite of my "little talks" with him to try and maintain the culture, he treated the matter like he treated the office staff—with impudence. "After all," he said, "I'm your biggest producer." If I think someone's out of line I'll tell them. I tried to convince him that if he'd tell me, I could tell them and try and resolve the situation, and that this would be the better approach. He disagreed, and from time to time he'd blow his stack at one of these assistants and call them on the carpet. What he didn't get was that later, when they had a chance to get even, they'd sabotage some piece of work or fail to leave a message. If he had just bought into the mission statement "treat the other person the way you want to be treated," he would have avoided a lot of heartburn and frustration, most of which was self-inflicted.

Jim Quigley is the CEO of Deloitte & Touche. Like Kevin Rollins and Rod Hawes, he conducts every aspect of his company's business with an eye toward total, unquestionable honesty and integrity.

After taking over as CEO of Deloitte & Touche, Jim Quigley staked out several strategic choices to frame the company's actions. Integrity is the accounting firm's first value. "I write and consistently reinforce in my speaking the importance of that value. We have to own the high ground. What's important is that our employees know that's how I am. The employees need to know and understand that integrity is what this organization values … When a client asks us to cut a corner, we won't do it. If they push us unmercifully, we resign. We just walk away."[21]

High trust and low fear must be the foundation of personal relationships. Total honesty, therefore, is not only the best policy, it is the only policy that builds lasting relationships with customers and employees. The arrogance that discredits or mocks adherence to such values is eventually uncovered, and it is often as ugly and costly as each of the scandals which rocked corporate America over the past several years.

Long before I completed my Chartered Life Underwriter degree, I was inspired by the professional pledge of those who graduate from the American College of Life Underwriters. The pledge is as follows:

"In all my professional relationships I pledge myself to

the following rule of ethical conduct. I shall, in the light of all conditions surrounding those I serve, which I shall make every conscious effort to ascertain and understand, render that service which, in the same circumstances, I would apply to myself."

Just think of the difference in peoples' lives and investments if Ken Lay and his top executives had treated his employees and investors the way this professional pledge requires. The fruits of doing it Enron's way were a total disaster.

The former Dean of the Harvard Business School, Kim Clark, speaking to a management group, tells a most interesting story:

"Unethical behavior starts out innocently enough. When materialism works its way into people's hearts, they begin to lose perspective. This can happen to anyone. But it isn't just materialism that has contributed to the ethics' decline. There are many factors affecting society's perspective on what's right and wrong. One of them is the educational system.

We're seeing the effects of decades of educational institutions abandoning their commitment to character development and to values as part of their missions. A kind of moral relativism has taken over and many faculty and administrators abandoned the idea that you should try to teach and develop students with character and honesty.

Part of the problem is the growing mentality that it doesn't matter what people's values are so long as they don't impose their ideology on others. If you preach that long enough, a lot of students come out of those kinds of schools believing it's true—that the idea of being honest (all the time) is just one group's view of what you should do. As a result, you get people who don't think very much about rules and certainly don't think the rules apply to them."[20]

In March 2005, Harvard Business School discovered that 119 of its applicants had hacked into a third-party Web site to get an early peek at their acceptance status, which had not yet been released by the school. In the midst of pressure, both from within and without the institution, Clark had to decide how HBS would react to such actions. It was decided to reject the guilty applicants. In his official statement, Clark said: "Our mission is to educate principled leaders who make a difference in the world. To achieve that, a person must have many skills and qualities, including the highest standards of integrity, sound judgment, and a strong moral compass—an intuitive sense of what is right and wrong. Those who have hacked into this Web site have failed to pass that test."[21]

Real leadership is not based on title, position, or the name on the door. Rather, it is a verb intended to identify how well one behaves when placed in positions of trust and responsibility. Real leadership already knows the answer to the question "what should I do?" and conducts itself accordingly. Real leadership demonstrates regularly that "you can trust me." Real leaders rarely have to say that, because they've already demonstrated trustworthiness through their actions and relationships with the "stakeholders" in the organization, as well as all of its clients and vendors.

This chapter concludes with words from Abraham Lincoln. It is sobering to ponder the great sadness of this truth in the lives of those who have lost their way morally.

"Nearly all men can stand adversity, but if you want to test a man's character, give him power."[22]

Here's the lesson:

- Integrity is a key part of the deal.
- The company will perform better if its employees are treated fairly and compensated appropriately.
- You can get more out of employees when you are good to them.
- Honesty is not only the best policy, it is the *only* policy that builds lasting relationships.

Chapter Sixteen

Understanding Business

*It's good to have pride in your accomplishments, but take care
that the pride doesn't overwhelm the accomplishment.*

—Peter S. Pande

Ram Charan is the ultimate mentor to some of this country's
best CEOs. In his book, *"What the CEO Wants You to Know,"* he
said: "When it comes right down to it, business is very simple.
There are universal laws of business that apply whether you
sell fruit from a stand or are running a Fortune 500 company.
Successful business leaders know them. They have what I
call business acumen—the ability to understand the building
blocks of how a one-person operation or a very big business
makes money.

The best CEOs and the man or woman running the
one-person shop think the same way. They know their cash
situation. They know which items are profitable and which are
not. They understand the importance of keeping their products
moving off the shelf ... and they know their customers."[23]

Great words, but what if you don't own the place? What

if you are hired to profitably manage the organization for the owners?

We observed that some people who don't own the company, but are hired to manage it for the owners, make the mistake of thinking like employees instead of employers, and they do only those specific tasks that are in their job description. On the other hand, some owners only want that kind of response from those that they hire to manage; they expect no entrepreneurial initiative from the hired help.

Developing the full potential of everyone working for you, whether you own the company or only manage it, is still based on exactly the same principles. In the development of our agency, we found that by tapping into that "untapped" entrepreneurial spirit of our best sales associates and helping them see that they were the boss and in charge of their own business, everything changed.

They began arriving at the office a little earlier and staying a little longer at the end of the day. They began to invest in their own business, and that investment was in equipment and systems that helped improve the speed and efficiency of case preparation. Their offices started looking more professional, and they hired additional secretarial help and worked out incentives for performance.

They got to the place where they stopped thinking like *employees* and started thinking like *employers*. They were two to three times more productive than those who were unable to make that paradigm shift.

Business ownership is really very simple. When our top associates realized how simple it was, they embraced the concept and became very successful at running their own businesses. When that happened, their production increased. As a result, we were more profitable than when *we* were the "boss" and *they* were "just insurance agents."

Does this kind of thinking work in every business out there? I don't know, but ponder this. Your best people have a specific job description. That job requires a planned profit margin. If they thought that their net compensation could increase based on increased productivity and profitability, is it likely that they would buy into that? It is likely, and when they do, it will be because they are treated like the "boss" of the area, or the territory, or the region over which they have responsibility.

I'm confident that some will say: "I'm not going to introduce that notion to my people. If I did, I'd be opening the door to everybody to leave and open their own shop. If they are the boss, they don't need me."

The only reason you'd want to worry about that possibility is if you are unprepared to provide them with the reasons to stay.

Our people stayed with us because we were, in essence, their business management consultants, who at the same time provided:

- Great office services
- Ongoing education
- The best marketing assistance they could find
- Financial incentives that they couldn't get anyplace else

Simply stated, when we provided these things, our

associates couldn't afford to leave us, even though they were autonomous in terms of conducting their business. The perks were too attractive, our leadership was too vital, but the key factor was treating them like they were the boss.

The preceding chapters in this book have examined the elements of the character of leadership. What you have read is a portrayal of things as they really are and is the result of what we actually did to create and maintain the best organization in our company's history. It's what we learned in the fire of managing our business like pros instead of like rookies. It's what we learned about leadership and checking our ego to be sure that "it's all about *them*, and not all about *me*." Any other kind of leadership lacks authenticity and cannot command the respect and loyalty of others.

That kind of loyalty is earned; it can never be demanded. You can earn it by helping your associates accomplish their potential. When they see the value of thinking and acting like business owners, everything about your career and theirs will change.

When they change the way they think about their career, they begin to take pride in the way they stick to the basics and get the big job done. As a result, they become more highly motivated to excel: they realize that they have the capacity to think and act like business people. When they are empowered by the fact that they own their area, they will become more productive than they were when they saw themselves only as employees.

To clarify, this doesn't work for every employee. It is only effective for your winners, for those who have an entrepreneurial nature and a fire in their gut.

When our top-quality people changed the way they saw the big picture and learned the basic principles of business success, they actually gained awareness. They became more aware of the opportunities and obstacles before them and began to act on values rather than reacting on emotions.

The business plan that each person created individually worked because they owned it. It was theirs. It was meaningful. And we had their permission to inquire regularly about their planned results. At the end of the year, if their planned performance was not up to the expectations *they* had set, the amount of financial assistance we were providing decreased. It was all up to them. They were the bosses, and we were the business management consultants. This reality gave them new reasons to get out of bed in the morning. It changed their paradigm of excellence.

That said, as you carry on the process of perfecting your own business plan, the ultimate motivation for your associates must still come from you. Be wise and avoid becoming one of those managers who finds it hard to share the applause or who finds it difficult to elevate subordinates. We got our accolades from the home office, but we always deferred to our exceptional group of winners, saying what a pleasure it was to be associated with such individuals.

In his book *Six Sigma Leader*, Peter Pande said: "An individual may be good at demanding high performance from his or her followers, or may have strong technical ability. However, those strengths are not sufficient when, for example, big-picture thinking or relationship building, are also essential to success. To prepare yourself and others for growing challenges, you need the clarity of thought and flexibility to understand your own weakness and develop new talents."[24]

Understanding the basics of business requires real leaders to understand their own strengths and weakness and never lose sight of the fundamental requirements that make an organization run.

Running it Like a Business

I didn't own the company. My associate managers and I were contracted to manage this assigned territory for the company. But what we were teaching our people is what we ourselves were doing. We were thinking and acting like we owned it all. As a result, we were successful because we carefully planned the basic necessities of our recruiting, training, marketing strategies, production goals, educational processes, sales promotion, real hard dollar costs, and total organizational culture. When we finally got to that place, we refused to deviate from those plans. We were very fortunate that we had the kind of energy and focus about our work that allowed us to stick to these tasks until they were completed. Persistency is an essential leadership trait.

We knew that our people would be successful when they did the things we told them to do. We knew it because prior to being in the world of agency building, the management team had all been very successful at marketing our products. We knew how to sell. We also knew how to design the case in such a way that it was uncluttered, straightforward, and very customer friendly. Presentations to the client that were designed in this manner could stand the scrutiny of "deal killers."

When your people learn to run their job like a business, they will accomplish more than either you or they ever thought possible.

Shaping and Defining It

The most important process we ever undertook in building our organization was the shaping and defining of organizational values.

Those clearly defined values were part of what made us different from our competitors.

And because we understood our business and spent the time, energy, and resources developing it, no agency in the company ever produced more winners than we did. Year after year, a large percentage of the leading agents in the company were from our organization. They were highly skilled; they knew where they were going and how they were going to get there. Those leading agents of ours were committed to regular, ongoing education, which allowed them to keep current with every facet of advanced markets and every change in tax law.

If You Don't Take Care of Your Customers, Somebody Else Will

We believed and constantly emphasized that the client was king. The way we treated our customers was at the forefront of what we did. One of the reasons we were always among the leading organizations in the company was because of client loyalty. We earned the right to that loyalty and were preoccupied with the necessity of it. We were focused on building client relationships that stayed glued. On rare occasions, there would be an associate who could not buy into that philosophy. When that happened, he got to find a new home.

Our clients were loyal to us and liked working with us because our relationship with them was based on the principle of treating them the way we wanted to be treated if the roles were reversed. With this client-centered mentality, our people grew very close to their clients. They gave service—especially after-the-sale service. They knew that the real sale was made after the sale was over. Their clients didn't forget them; instead, they bought from them again and again.

Those companies that are not focused on client relationships are destined to show "short-term" performance, shooting-star bursts of light, but precious little long-term staying power. You really have two choices in business, and it makes no difference whether you're selling insurance, financial services, computer software, or Mack trucks. In your career, you can have thirty years of experience, or you can have one year of experience repeated thirty times. It is up to you.

All of the universal laws of success apply to every business. When we understand our customers and our products as well as these universal laws, our success will be without limits. The surprise is that when it comes to running businesses successfully, the small self-employed vendor of any product and the CEOs of some of the largest and most successful companies really do talk and think alike.

If you're not sure about all these principles, don't worry:

- That which you persist in doing actually will become easier for you to do.

- Be wise and get away from lame excuses like "I don't have time to do all this."

- There's plenty of time to fix it, but never enough time to do it right the first time.

- Time is not the problem. Lack of will and focus is.

- Take steps to find out what the best companies and their leaders do. When you learn what that is, then decide what you need to do to change the way you operate.

- Prepare the road map, establish the mission statement, and start the process.

- Be brave, and you will never be the same.

As the renowned historian James Harvey Robinson said: "Greatness, in the last analysis, is largely bravery—courage in escaping from old ideas and old standards and respectable ways of doing things. This is one of the chief elements in what we vaguely call capacity. If you do not dare to differ from your associates and teachers, you will never be great or your life sublime. You may be the happier as a result, or you may be miserable. Each of us is great insofar as we perceive and act on the infinite possibilities which lie undiscovered and unrecognized about us."[25]

The things we did in building our exceptional organization were based on a combination of doing what the best did, developing a winning culture, and a lot of common sense. It's not nearly as mind-bending as you might think, but it does require you to change. So start. You can do it if you want to! Dream it, plan it, gather winners around you that have a fire for greatness and accomplishment, and move forward by making your purpose greater than your moods. It is glorious to be an exception.

Here's the lesson:

- The best CEO's and the man running the one-person shop think the same way.
- When your people stop thinking like *employees* and start thinking like *employers*, they will become two to three times more productive.
- Make your relationship with your associates consultative.
- Reel in your ego so that you can assure that it's not all about *you,* because it really is all about *them.*

Notes

1 Gray, Albert E.N."The Common Denominator of Success." National Association of Life Underwriters Annual Meeting, 1940.

2 Grant, Heber. "LDS Conference Report," April 1921, p.63.

3 Huntsman, Jon M. *Winners Never Cheat*, Wharton School Publishing, 2005.

4 Nibley, Hugh. "Management Vs. Leadership," BYU Commencement Address, April 1983.

5 Twain, Mark.

6 Tracy, Brian. *Courageous Leadership*, GAMA News Journal, March 1996.

7 *Management Review vol. 50*, "The Ill-informed Walrus," American Management Association, October 1961.

8 Shelton, Ken. *A New Paradigm For Leadership*, Executive Excellence Publishing, 1997.

9 Benedict, Jeff. "Faith, flight plan guide JetBlue Boss: Other CEOs need his humility," Boston Herald, March 5, 2007.

10 Porter, David Dr. "David O. McKay Lecture," BYU, Hawaii, February 2007.

11 Gardner, Peter B. *BYU Magazine*, Winter 2007.

12 From personal notes taken at "Covey Leadership Week," February 1986.

13 McAlpine, Ken. "The Energizer," *Southwest Spirit*, February 2001.

14 Clark, Kim. "Learning is the Key," *Deseret News*, May 2007.

15 Collins, Jim. *Good to Great*, p.120, HarperCollins, 2001.

16 Welch, Jack. *Winning*, p.37, Harper Business, 2005.

17 Fiffer, Jules. As quoted in a talk by Ed Fendt, Million Dollar Round Table Annual Meeting, June, 1971.

18 McCarthy, Robert J. Rev. Funeral service for Wayne Estes, February 1965.

19 Hillel was a Jewish Rabbi of royal bloodline who lived at the time of Herod the Great. The quote has been passed down and enhanced by many speakers.

20 From *The Mormon Way of Doing Business* by Jeff Benedict. Copyright (c 2007 by Jeff Benedict Enterprises LLC. By permission of Grand Central Publishing.

21 Clark Kim. "Personal Ethics," *Deseret News*, Church News Section, July 28, 2007.

22 Lincoln, Abraham. *Thoughts on Leadership*, Triumph Books, 1995.

23 Charan, Ram. *What the CEO Wants You to Know*, Crown Business, 2001.

24 Pande, Peter S. *The Six Sigma Leader*, McGraw Hill, 2007, p.31.

25 Robinson, James Harvey. *Thoughts on Leadership*, Triumph Books, 1995.

www.ingramcontent.com/pod-product-compliance
Lightning Source LLC
Chambersburg PA
CBHW032019170526
45157CB00002B/773